Romain Goldron

MINSTRELS AND MASTERS

H. S. Stuttman Company, Inc., Publishers
Distributed by Doubleday & Company, Inc.

Designed by Erik Nitsche

HISTORY
OF
MUSIC

3

1   *Juggler. (English—late 14th century)*

Contents

2-3 *The jugglers were actors and dancers as well as traveling musicians.*
Here, one plays the flute and the drum. (English—late 15th century)

The 10th century marked the end of the true Middle Ages. In all fields the 11th century was a turning point, and in music it marked the first hesitant steps toward sophisticated composition, heralding the modern age.

The 12th century gave birth to the lyricism of the troubadours, the chronicle and the romance. It saw the renaissance of early literature, the first experiments in polyphony, seeking to escape the single melodic strain of early composition, and the emergence of a sacred drama. It has been called the century of the Second Renaissance, which brought to maturity the fruits of the Carolingian Renaissance three hundred years before.

But it is the 13th century that concerns us now. It was the age of Gothic purity, courtly romance in literature, minstrels, German ballad singers, the school of Notre-Dame and the glory of counterpoint.

A New Class of Musicians

There is one class of musicians about whose early experiences little is known. In the 13th century, however, they begin gradually to emerge from the shadows to which the prejudice of the Church had confined them, and to form themselves into officially recognized brotherhoods and take their place in history.

7

4 Distant descendants of the wandering shaman, the jugglers and the minstrels maintained a primitive magical order, hence the animal disguises and the hostility of the Church. Left, beaked flute.

5 *Psaltery, bagpipes, horn and bells
in the letter X of the grotesque alphabet.
Engraving by P. Langlois.*

5

The growth of secular music—which we can consider only in broad outline since few texts, if any, have survived to permit detailed study—is inseparable from the story of these musicians. To consider the reconciliation between the vocal music of the Church and the instrumental music of lay origin—so long outlawed by religious authority—it is essential to have some idea of the history of the minstrels and the jugglers. They were more general entertainers than their modern counterparts. It is important that we know about their organization, their repertoire and their role in music. Recent studies have made this possible.[1]

Origins

The existence of a class of traveling musicians, either singers or instrumentalists, or both, is by no means confined to the Middle Ages. From earliest times—and until quite recently—actors, bards and musicians have taken to the road, traveling from town to town, from castle to castle. They were distant descendants of the wandering shaman—a combination of healer, clairvoyant and singer—of Asia. The same kind of medicine-man figure was well known in Africa and North America. Often the shaman, the bard, and sometimes even the traveling player, were one and the same person.

From the beginning, song and sorcery went hand in hand. Odin was master of mystic and heroic song alike. The same close links existed in Finland. In 6th-century Greece, strolling minstrels doubled as fortune-tellers. The *spielmann,* or minstrel, of the Middle Ages frequently supplemented his gifts as an instrumentalist with a talent for soothsaying. These ties between song and the old mystic traditions explain the hostility of the Church toward the traveling musicians, the constant warnings and interdictions throughout the Middle Ages.

On the other hand, courts both great and small of all ages have found a need for singers, poets and musicians. They were called upon to extol the glory and virtue of princes and potentates and to proclaim the grandeur of the court and its pretensions. But they were entertainers, too, needed to add color at banquets and other festive occasions.

As a rule, singers and musicians were not attached to a particular court or castle; rather, they wandered from place to place, just as the modern entertainer flits from performance to performance in different parts of the world. Their reward—and nothing has changed in this respect, either—depended on both their skill and their popularity, and the size of the reward could vary considerably. Their status, too, varied from period to

9

6   7

period. In ancient times they were often held as slaves; slave musicians were offered for sale in Rome as late as A.D. 385.

It is to this class of traveling musicians that the juggler, the minstrel and the spielmann of the Middle Ages belong.

The term "juggler" comes from the Latin *joculator,* meaning one who brings laughter, and by extension, relaxation. In France he was the *jongleur,* in Italy the *giocolore* or *giullare.* "Minstrel" also has a Latin base— *ministerialis,* meaning a minor official. Its etymology suggests that the minstrel was a traveling musician who had abandoned the road for a permanent post, but the word has had different meanings for different chroniclers. One 14th-century French definition sees the minstrels as musicians, in the sense of instrumentalists, and describes them as players of drums, the psaltery, the horn, the guitar, the flute or the vielle. But the word has a wider meaning for other writers.

One writer talks of "trumpeters," "minstrels" (*ménestriers*) and "players of instruments," drawing a clear distinction. But the French poet Chrétien de Troyes, writing in the 12th century, apparently viewed the minstrel and the juggler as one and the same. It is perhaps significant that in Paris a "rue des Jugléeurs" of the 14th century should have been renamed the "rue des Ménestriers."

6-8 Preceding pages: Performers on the vielle, the monochord and the mandola. The monochord is not to be confused with the triangular marine trumpet (or tromba marina), although both instruments had a single string (very occasionally, two strings). It barely survived as far as the Middle Ages. The mandola (or mandora), an instrument of the lute family, is pear-shaped; its peg-box curves backward like a sickle.
9 Man playing the bagpipes. Fragment of a 15th-century German tapestry showing the hunt for a unicorn. The bagpipes were known to Mesopotamian civilization and reached Europe from Asia in about the 1st century A.D. They have remained popular in certain areas, including Scotland and the Bohemian region of Czechoslovakia.
10 Following pages: All the ideals of the Middle Ages are symbolized in this 14th-century German painting: service to God, chivalry and homage to womanhood. The learned art of music is consecrated to God; troubadours, minnesingers and mastersingers extol love in their songs, while minstrels and jugglers entertain the nobility and bring to their courts the musical glory they require.

12

11

There are few contemporary descriptions of the Celto-Germanic world before the 4th century A.D. But the evidence from that time on suggests that the musicians were divided into two very distinct classes. One, the scops, or Germanic bards, belonged to the nobility. The other, the *joculators,* came from lower down the social ladder.

The Nordic nations, from Iceland to Denmark, were the territory of the *scaldes.* Theirs was an aristocratic art and a feature of that area throughout the Middle Ages. Like their counterparts farther south, they were traveling performers and appeared at the courts of all the countries around the North Sea, including the English court. They were often found in the royal retinue when a king set out on an expedition.

Their art was at its height in the 11th century—a century before Sweden's conversion to Christianity—and the names of more than two hundred of them are recorded in the literature of the period. They sang their epics without instrumental accompaniment, and they maintained a proud independence from the *gliman,* the Nordic actor or mime.

The distinction was less in Germany, where the term spielmann (literally, "he who plays") embraced all the performers from about the 8th century on. It included the joculator, the mime, the *histrio*—a type of actor, almost certainly a dancer or a herald at first—as well as the scop. The spielmann's profession was not limited solely to males, but the women who ventured to join could count on little praise from the medieval middle classes.

The unity of the performing classes was not to last, however, and by the 14th century trumpeters, drummers, singers and organists were refusing to regard themselves as part of the spielmann movement. It was, to them, a term of affront and insult.

Whatever their social status, it is clear that in the Middle Ages there were groups of itinerant musicians in every part of Europe, extending from the Christian regions in the south to the still pagan or newly converted Nordic regions. To ignore this fact and to consider the history of music in the Middle Ages as the history of Christian religious music alone is to glimpse only part of the picture. The constant journeyings of these musicians and the wide contacts they made were in part responsible for the creation of a unified musical culture in the West and paved the way for the development of a truly European language of music.

The journeys could be long. The Germanic bard who is the hero of the old English poem "Wîdsîth" was supposed to have visited seventy-two countries, including even the Indies! The poem speaks of his singing to his own accompaniment on

12

the harp. Sometimes he was joined by a second instrumentalist, and they would sing together, or perhaps in turn.

At the court of Attila the Hun two singers were hired for "table music."[2] Priskas, the Byzantine ambassador to Attila's court in 446, left an account showing that the singers were not necessarily the only performers. On one occasion, he noted, the program was opened by two Scythian bards, who sang the praises of heroic virtue. They were followed by a joculator engaged for his wit. Finally, on came an African dwarf. It was a program common enough in all the medieval courts.

Not that the entertainers confined themselves to performances at court. The convents of the Middle Ages, and even the higher echelons of the clergy, regarded the actors as welcome visitors, much to the anger of the Church.

The Council of Aquileia declared in 791, ". . . all the worldly honors to which the people of this age and the princes of the earth are accustomed, such as hunting, secular song, endless and immoderate rejoicings . . . should not be part of the way of life of the servants of the Church. . . ."

The Council of Tours in 813 warned priests to avoid the "immodesties of dishonest actors and their obscene amusements."

Less than thirty years later, the Bishop of Or-léans deemed it necessary to issue further instructions. He banned the singing of "rustic poems" and the staging of "indecent" performances by female dancers at gatherings in a presbytery.

Instructions and interdictions of this kind, even excommunication or refusal of communion for some itinerant musicians, continued throughout the Middle Ages. These were a direct reflection of the activity of the minstrels and the actors.

Music and Dancing

A striking feature of contemporary accounts and ecclesiastical reports is the close association between music and dancing in the sacred as well as in the secular fields.

The Council of Avignon declared in 1209: "We have decreed that at the vigils of the saints [held on the eve of important religious festivals] there should not be, in the churches, any of this theatrical dancing, these immodest rejoicings, these meetings of singers with their worldly songs, which incite the souls of those who hear them to sin."

Three years later came this from the Council of Paris: "Gatherings of women for the purpose of dancing and singing shall not be granted permission to enter cemeteries or to tread on consecrated ground. . . ."

13

"Nuns will not set themselves at the head of processions which sing and dance on the rounds of churches and their chapels . . . for according to St. Gregory it is better to plough and to dig on the Sabbath than to conduct these dances. . . ."

The reference to St. Gregory, who lived centuries earlier, is in itself a commentary on the persistence of the old Church traditions.

In the 13th century, at the Council of Bayeux, the message was the same. "Priests will forbid gatherings for dancing and singing in churches and cemeteries, on pain of excommunication."

The steadfastly negative attitude of Church officialdom can be interpreted as an indication of how little the warnings were being heeded.

The 14th-century German mystics, such as Heinrich Suso and Hildegard von Bingen, could not conceive of a heaven without "dances of joy" to the "sweet airs of the pipe of Christ." And German spiritual airs of the 15th century portray Jesus as master of heavenly dancing, with behind him a troupe of holy maidens striking drums and playing the vielle or the flute.[3]

One fact is clear from all the texts that have survived. In the words of Manfred Bukofzer, professor of music at the University of California, Berkeley, until his death in 1955, dancing was "a fundamental activity of medieval life, not only in the market place and at local secular festivals, but also—and this is more surprising—in the church."

The epidemic of dancing that spread over the whole of Europe at the end of the Middle Ages, Bukofzer states, took the form of the *danse macabre,* the dance of death, and the *danse de St. Guy.* The last-named seems to have been similar to what is termed St. Vitus' dance, and several texts refer to its ecstatic character. But, Bukofzer adds, "We know virtually nothing of the music of these dances."[4]

For a proper understanding of the situation, it is important to remember that the dividing line between affairs secular and affairs sacred was still fluid in the Middle Ages. Dances in the church, in the cemetery or in the processions were a continuation of ritual dances that had strong roots in tradition. It took the Church centuries of protest to gain its objective.

No matter what the Church said, the fact is that certain liturgical texts make explicit mention of the dances of the cantor and the young monks, and according to one authority,[5] even refer to dances to the Gregorian chants, "which had not been composed for that purpose."

The dances were staged particularly at Christmas, Easter and Pentecost—in other words, to coincide with the midwinter, midsummer and spring

19

16

17

solstices, which all religions have always celebrated in dance and song.

The Work of the Jugglers

The jugglers, the minstrels and their kind staged their performances in a number of different settings.

Despite protests from the highest authorities, the Church was unable to effect a united front against them. Many bishops tolerated their presence during major festivals or royal visits. Some, indeed, even had minstrels and singers as part of their own households.

It is to be remembered that many senior members of the clergy were at the same time aristocrats and of noble birth. When they moved to their abbeys or to their official palaces they were loth to leave behind them all the trappings of the court. From the time of Charlemagne there is ample evidence of rich and powerful princes of the Church maintaining musicians to add splendor and status to their offices. By the 13th century there was scarcely one in Europe who was without his jugglers or his players.[6] Pope Leo X created a veritable troupe of entertainers for himself, and the monasteries greeted them as welcome visitors.

With a few outstanding exceptions—Henry IV of England, Philippe-Auguste of France and Rudolph I of Hapsburg were examples—the lords and sovereigns of Europe maintained a high regard for the jugglers and minstrels. And if some noblemen were without the generous spirit, there were plenty of others to provide reward enough to a successful entertainer.

They were paid in goods—food, clothing and horses. Money came infrequently, and more than one juggler had occasion to deplore the ingratitude of his host:

> *Sire, I have played*
> *Before you in your mansion,*
> *Yet have you given me nothing*
> *To meet my debts at the tavern.*
> *It is meanness. . . .*
>
> Colin Muset[7]

Otto III, ruler of the Holy Roman Empire at the end of the 10th century, Frederic III of Germany, Archbishop von Dassel of Cologne, Richard I of England, Louis IX of France, the kings of Sweden, the Spanish regents of the 14th and 15th centuries, Philippe III of France and the kings of Bohemia in Prague all left behind them reputations of great generosity toward traveling musicians.

18 Dulcimer player. The strings were struck with small hammers, producing a dry, metallic sound. The dulcimer was the forerunner of the cimbalon, which is still in use among the Hungarian gypsies.

18

The treatment any particular entertainer could expect depended, of course, upon his skill and his popularity. As a rule, the entertainers were lodged in the servants' quarters, but some—in particular, the troubadours and the minnesingers—received extremely high consideration. The most sought-after minstrels were assured not only rich rewards but also a place of honor at the table.

There was a distinction between the performer pure and simple—the man who contented himself with the existing repertoire—and the creative artist who could present songs, dances and music of his own composition. And just as talent establishes its own order of merit today, so then. An informal, but nevertheless clear, hierarchy existed.

At the top stood the minstrels of the *chansons de geste,* the heroic epic poems that represented some of the best literature of the time. After them came the trumpeters, the drummers and the timpani players, who formed the aristocracy of the profession. It was the ambition of every minstrel and juggler to graduate to one of these fields.

The eminence of the trumpet sprang from its long and close association with royal power. From earliest times it was the instrument *par excellence* of glory, power and domination. A royal residence without trumpets or drums was, to a medieval observer, incomplete.

It was the sound of trumpets that heralded the arrival of princes—royal and of the Church—at a town or a castle. And the degree of power a nobleman possessed could be judged by the number of his trumpeters as much as by their costumes and the richness of the pennants that hung below their instruments.

Ministrels had the right to play only the "minstrels' trumpet"—the trombone. Trumpeters, therefore, were relatively few. They rode on horseback, like the knights. They took part in all major pageants—the tournaments, the marriages, the great receptions. Competition for a place in their ranks was understandably keen.

As the middle class increased in importance, the towns were accorded the privilege of retaining their own trumpeters. But a strict watch was maintained to see that their performances were reserved for the exclusive pleasure of the nobility and the middle class.

Officially, weddings among the lower classes were supposed to take place without the benefit of a trumpet accompaniment. But the number of decrees warning against the misuse of trumpets at "minor" marriages suggests that the musicians were not averse to "persuasion." On such occasions, of course, they risked sharing the platform with a very low class of juggler!

19

19 *"A garden crowded with
animals, such as were pictured
in royal entryways." In the center of the
garden a young man, a medieval Orpheus,
plays the vielle. (18th-century document)*

There were, of course, no concerts at which a musician might display his talents. The concert is quite a modern concept, and the medieval alternatives reveal just how large a part the minstrels and the jugglers played in the everyday life of the Middle Ages.

A nobleman planning a major journey could assure himself of some distraction on his long, monotonous travels by taking along a few jugglers able to sing the fashionable songs, to tell stories and fables and to engage him in conversation. Some even took their jugglers to church with them, and made friends and even confidants of them. It goes without saying that no nobleman ever set off to war or on a pilgrimage without his jugglers.

The arrival of a group of jugglers and minstrels could create considerable excitement in a castle, where life—these establishments were often built some distance from the nearest town—tended to be monotonous.

Gaston Phebus, a 14th-century nobleman, whose home was a castle high in the Pyrenees, recorded the program of his average day: "Hunting; after the hunt, Mass; after Mass, the womenfolk and the minstrels."[8] The pattern must have been familiar in château society.

A ball, the arrival of a distinguished guest, a tournament, any kind of ceremonial whether inspired by the happy prospect of a marriage, or by the solemnity attending a formal induction into knighthood—all these were occasions for the talents of jugglers. At a festival they would appear in force at the herald's summons, in all kinds of guises. Some, magnificently dressed, might be on horseback; others on foot, clothed in rags.

In formal processions they would accompany the important personages, or march at the head. They were always present at mealtimes, marking the successive courses with music.

"At the wedding celebrations of Robert d'Artois, brother of St. Louis [Louis IX of France], two jugglers, mounted on bulls decked in purple, sounded a trumpet fanfare at each new dish," wrote Edmond Faral, one of the leading modern authorities on life in medieval France.[9]

There may be some exaggeration in the following description of an after-dinner entertainment by the author of the 13th-century romance *Flamenca*, but its details are certainly accurate:

"When the meal was over, the guests cleansed themselves and then took wine, without leaving their seats. Mirrors were brought in, that each could order himself as he pleased. And then, on came the jugglers, each anxious to win favor. You would have heard instruments of all kinds. Whoever knew a new air on the viol, a song, a lyric or

20-21 *Among the minstrels the trumpeters,
the drummers and the timpanists formed the
aristocracy of the profession. They rode
on horseback and enjoyed special privileges.*
(Chronicle of Bertrand de Guesclin, *1320-1380*)

21

22

a lay struggled to push himself forward. One played the lay of the honeysuckle on his viol, another the lay of Tintagel; one sang of the faithful lovers, another the lay of Ivan; one played the harp, another the viol; one the flute, another the fife; one played a *giga* [an early type of fiddle], another the *hrotta* [a kind of lyre] from Brittany; one played the musette, another the pipe; one the bagpipes, another the recorder; one the mandola, another the one-stringed psaltery. One danced puppets, another juggled with knives; one slithered on the ground, another turned somersaults. . . ."

Inns and hostelries, like the numerous dancing establishments, offered the jugglers a natural opportunity to earn a little money by entertaining the visitors.

"If there is one pleasure which is tasted by all," comments Faral,[10] "and which appeals to all classes of society, it is dancing." Sometimes the dances were performed by jugglers—male or female. One of their most popular numbers was called *Herodias,* which was something of a stage production in miniature, featuring a female dancer as Salome. Usually, however, everybody danced.

In the country, dancing took place in the meadow or in the village square under the trees. Urban society preferred the spacious rooms of the Town Hall usually reserved for weddings and dancing. In Paris people went to Saint-Germain on Sundays to dance. Faral says they would dance in the streets—day and night—on any excuse. He points out that dancing was also one of the most favored amusements of high society.

In the salons, dances of a dramatic character were the rage. The dancers would depict a scene, or tell a story such as this one, the dance of the "flower rosary," as related by Faral:[11]

"Four men present a lady before the audience. They place her on a seat, where she plays with a crown of flowers she holds in her hand. A minstrel asks here why she sits there, all alone, without companions and without friends. She replies with a song, and then, still talking to the minstrel, she takes her garland of flowers, places it on her head, removes it again and then replaces it. Finally she dances towards an imaginary grove, where she continues dancing until the minstrel brings to her a young man, who pleases her and leads her off, both singing."

In the *danse robardoise* a dancer in shepherd's clothes "leaps and jigs to please a young girl who seeks to avoid him but from whom, by surprise, he steals a kiss."

Another popular dance was the *carole*—a term applied both to the dance and to the song to which it was performed. Caroles were dancing songs

23

born in aristocratic circles and passed on by word of mouth. Sometimes they took the form of a rondeau or a virelai. The dance was performed either to unaccompanied singing or to instrumental music and was under the direction of a leader, who shared the singing with the other dancers.

Jugglers and minstrels were also to be found in large numbers in the spas, the bathing establishments that are such a curious feature of the Middle Ages, a period of bursting health in which the most elevated spirituality and the purest asceticism went hand in hand with the greatest freedom in speech and in customs.

In both Germany and France the baths were a popular meeting place, and they were many. At Heilbronn, for example, there was a spa for every thousand people. Paris had twenty-six separate spas in 1292.

Men and women shared the bath and, in the warm relaxing water, listened together to the minstrels and the jugglers, who wandered in and out of the bathhouse or sat on the window ledges. The lute and the flute were the favorite instruments. Patrons of the baths could receive massages and have their hair dressed. They could sleep there, eat there and drink there.

The *Roman de la Rose,* one of the best-known medieval romantic poems, written in the first half of the 13th century, displays no sense of shock when it mentions the young men and women "who take walks in the meadows and the gardens and afterwards take themselves to the baths, where they bathe together, wearing floral garlands upon their heads." It was the custom.

The jugglers were closely associated with public life in the cities. At the election of the burgomaster, at civil ceremonies and at marriages the presence of musicians was required. At haymaking and harvest time, they escorted the reapers as far as the gates of the town.

Then there were the common people, poor perhaps, but a loyal and deserving public for all that. At the fairs they listened with equal satisfaction to jugglers recounting the lives of the saints beside pilgrim sanctuaries and to those telling ribald stories.

"No middle class or peasant wedding took place without jugglers to lead the bridal procession to church and to liven up the marriage feast," writes Faral. On feast days "they accompanied the town sergeants as they walked the streets by torchlight." A celebration of any kind would find them at the homes of merchants and tradesmen.[12]

Acrobats, dancers and snake-charmers enjoyed the same popularity as the singers and the storytellers. There was yet another group of jugglers

24   *Juggler. (English—15th century)*
25   *Group of jugglers and minstrels*
performing near a mill. (woodcut from
a work on the Influence of the Planets, *1470;*
Print Museum, Berlin)

24

whose specialty was—to use a modern term—current affairs.

These particular jugglers were the precursors of our modern journalists and our political satirists. Sometimes princes made use of their talents, as when Richard Lionheart paid jugglers to sing his praises in public squares. But they were not always dependent on patronage, and they frequently took part in the debates currently holding public interest. In their satire and in their humor, and sometimes in their laments, they echoed the mood of the ordinary man in the street, who would take up their songs as his own.

The Chanson de Geste

For a long time the minstrels of the *chanson de geste* occupied a special position in the brotherhood of the traveling musicians. They traveled on horseback and enjoyed great respect in the castles they visited—the same respect that was accorded everywhere to the bard, the singer of the old epic poems.

With the decline of knighthood, however, and the development of a town-based, middle-class society, the prestige of the epic and of its poets began to decline. The bards were reduced to reciting their poems before the masses, whereas once they had sung them in the great castles in a place of honor. In France this process was already taking place during the 13th century, but in Hungary the epic minstrel retained his position for another two hundred years, and in Russia until comparatively recent times.

The greatest of the chansons de geste, the *Song of Roland,* was written in France between 1080 and 1100. It was one of a line of French epic poems. Now it is primarily regarded as a work of literature. Nevertheless, it was written to be sung, and as such, it has a definite place in the history of music.

The epic poems were extremely long—ranging from 5,000 to 10,000 lines. Unfortunately, none of the music to which they were sung has survived, and opinions differ on the way the minstrels performed these immense works. One school of thought believes that each strophe, or stanza, was recited on the same note, like a litany, with the exception of a cadence on the last line. Others, however, suggest that the singers employed three different tones: one in the introductory passage, another in the main body of the poem and a third at the conclusion. The minstrel accompanied himself, probably on a vielle—a forerunner of the violin—or on a harp, or supported the rhythm of the poem with a drum.

The lay, another form of narrative poem, took its subjects from ancient Celtic legend. No primitive lay has survived, and the works of this form composed later (one of the best-known authors was the 12th-century Norman poet, Marie de France), although they do adopt the primitive themes, have more of a lyrical than a narrative character.

Vagabond Poets

Despite the fact that they are sometimes grouped with the jugglers and the players, the vagabond poets, or *goliards,* actually formed a class of their own. Their very background set them apart.

The goliards were students, with a few more or less unfrocked monks, traveling from one university to another. They went from abbey to tavern and from tavern to abbey, where their irreverence and brashness did little to enhance their reputation. They earned their living by tavern appearances, hence the confusion with the jugglers. But their racy repertoire, part in Latin, part in the vernacular, was unique, striking in its truculence and its humor. Examples of their art have survived to the present day. The German composer Carl Orff set some of their songs to music in his *Carmina Burana* in 1937.

In Beauvais, France, in 1140 these light-hearted student brotherhoods staged what was, in effect, a full-blown musical drama, the *Jeu de Daniel* (The Story of Daniel). It involved dialogue, songs, musicians, ballet, and it had an elaborate setting. Indeed, it was not far removed from an as yet unthought of medium, opera.

"Scholae Mimorum"

The wide diversity of the public that the jugglers set out to entertain and the variety of occasions at which they were invited to appear imply a highly developed adaptability, and in addition, an enormous repertoire—which, it should be remembered, was not written down.

Where, then, did the jugglers, the minstrels and the players find their material? Where did they learn the skills of their profession? For although there were second-rate performers and beggars among them, it is obvious that the élite of the profession—the men whom kings, princes and noblemen were prepared to receive and to reward—understood at the very least the rudiments of musical and poetic technique.

To make a good impression on his audience, a juggler had to be up to date—at all times. He had to know the songs currently in vogue, songs fre-

32

populus   romanus

Callinus

Theatrum   Theatrum

Ioculatores

quently designed for dancing, moreover. The absence of any swift means of transport did not deter people from traveling, and exotic reminders of foreign lands, the songs and airs of distant countries, were in high demand. The royal feasts in Dresden, for example, took their themes from ancient mythology, from the Old Testament, from the animal fables, and from foreign countries with unfamiliar traditions.[13]

A beginner had three avenues open to him to learn the skills and the material of his art. He could simply imitate the jugglers he saw and heard. He could accompany a master juggler as an apprentice and receive lessons. Or he could take instruction at a *schola mimorum,* a school for jugglers, particularly in the 14th and 15th centuries.

The schools were held in conjunction with the great assemblies of jugglers. They met generally during Lent, a slack period for the profession; on the occasion of a large fair, which might last as long as six weeks in an important center; or during the great councils of the Church. (The Councils of Constance and Basel in the 15th century lasted several years and brought together the elite, temporal and spiritual, of all Christianity.) On such occasions the student jugglers found the opportunity to perfect their skills under the supervision of

the masters of the profession, who gave them what amounted to a true education.

For the professionals themselves, these gatherings provided an opportunity for fruitful contacts and exchanges—exchanges of songs, of dances and even of instruments they might have brought back from journeys to other countries. The schools at Paris and Beauvais in France and at Tournai in Belgium were particularly renowned, and some noblemen sent their minstrels to them to renew their repertoires.

Beginners were able to learn all the tricks of the trade—how to vary the motif of a dance, how to improvise, and how to play musical instruments, which some, at least, mastered with considerable virtuosity.

The minstrel schools were born of a need for organization. From the end of the 13th century, there is actual evidence that the minstrels formed themselves into religious associations. The move was designed, perhaps, merely to improve their social condition, but it is also possible to see in this accession to social order the results of a change in attitude toward them, an official recognition of their activity.

The oldest of the minstrel brotherhoods, that of St. Nicholas in Vienna, dates from 1288. In 1355 the Holy Roman Empire officially recognized a

30 *Portrait of the minnesinger Oswald von Wolkenstein.*
(Tyrolean school—15th century)
31 *This figure, from a 14th-century treatise on astrology, holds an instrument of the lute family, but probably symbolic. The tripartite form of the instrument's body may be a reference to the three worlds, or classes, of music of the medieval theoreticians:* Musica mundana*(cosmic),* musica humana *and* musica intrumentalis.

Rex omnium histrionum—(King of all the minstrels). This minstrel king, named by Emperor Charles IV himself, was one Hans der Fiedler. (His name is the same word as "fiddler," applied to any player of a stringed instrument.) Strasbourg had its *Confrérie de la Couronne* (Brotherhood of the Crown), whose king was chosen by the lords of Rappoltstein. In Switzerland the right of election belonged to the Count of Kyburg, and later to his heirs, the city of Zurich.

The same thing was happening in France. In 1295 King Philippe IV named one Jean Charmillon "king of the minstrels." The first Parisian brotherhood was founded in 1321 by twenty-nine minstrels and eight women jugglers. They had their own chapel, Saint-Julien-des-Ménestriers, as St. Julian was their patron saint, and a hostel for their older members.[14]

Figures are lacking on the number of minstrels and their like, for obvious reasons, but there must have been many. A few isolated figures mentioned in various texts give some indication of the quantity involved.

One Italian town is said to have entertained a gathering of 1,500 jugglers in 1324. There were four hundred at the court of Mantua in 1340; in 1460, of Vienna's population of about 25,000, five hundred were classed as Jews and jugglers.[15]

Influence of the Jugglers

A study of the principal routes taken by the jugglers reveals the cosmopolitan makeup of the Middle Ages and shows how great was the urge to travel. For the jugglers were not alone on the roads.

There were merchants, students and monks. There were the groups involved in the Crusades. There were long and elaborate pilgrimages and numerous processions, like those of the flagellants —a fanatical sect who publicly whipped themselves—traveling the length and breadth of Christendom. There were the knights, with their constant journeyings. And underlying all this were the centuries of unbroken migration that had created a legacy of instability and that impelled the people of the Middle Ages on to the roads.

The same instability, by fostering contacts between peoples, was in part responsible for the development of a "United Europe"—a single cultural if not political entity. And the jugglers played an active role in it all. It is through them that so many European countries have a common popular foundation for their music and their legends. They were responsible for the spread of many instruments. They were the curators of the ancient traditions that linked the Middle Ages to a distant past.

32

Despite the incessant and active opposition of the Church, the jugglers maintained and developed in the West the use of musical instruments and the taste for instrumental groups, laying vital foundations for the future growth of European music. It is this that gives them an unchallenged and essential place in the history of music, even though they left no legacy of written music. They were the tillers of the soil and the sowers of seed, and the fruit of their labors was an instrumental music that embodied the profound liking for dancing in the Middle Ages. The *estampies* of the late 13th century, a dance form that provided the first examples of purely instrumental composition, were the cautious vanguard of that music.

The minstrels had already begun occasionally to form themselves into instrumental groups—large or small according to circumstances. The instruments they used are featured in the illustrations in this volume. A combination of flute and drum, or kettledrum, was popular. Other combinations were two trumpets; the harp and the vielle; the pipe and the bagpipes; the pipe, the *bombardon* (a forerunner of the tuba) and the trombone; and the portative organ and three string instruments, usually the vielle, the lute and the harp. Contemporary engravings and manuscripts provide evidence of larger groupings, whose composition seems to have

been flexible, largely depending on the instruments available.

The Motet

The motet—not to be confused with the 16th-century religious compositions of the same name—reached its peak in the mid-13th century. It owed its development to the work of two men who followed each other as precentor at the Cathedral of Notre Dame in Paris, although neither is known to have written anything in this form. The renown of these two composers, Leoninus and Perotinus, was founded on the *organum* and the *clausula,* forms that became particularly associated with the cathedral.

The organum, which was at its height toward the end of the 12th century, was a form of composition in which a second part was imposed on the plain-chant voice, creating the first examples of true polyphony. The clausula was a clearly defined contrapuntal section within the organum, which reached its highest development in the early 13th century.

In the motet, words (in French, *mots,* hence the name) were put to the vocalized upper part of the organum, one syllable to each note. At first the words were simply a paraphrase of the *teneur,*

40

33

the plain-chant base. But it was not long before the teneur began to lose its importance, to be sung only in part, and then not at all. It was entrusted to an instrument—a vielle, a psaltery or a portative organ. The second part, however, the motet proper, began to develop in an ever more independent fashion. Soon a third voice was added above the motet, and the word came to mean both the composition as a whole and the voice part above the teneur. The third voice was termed the *triplum*, and if a fourth voice was added on top of that, it was the *quadruplum*.

The strange thing, at least at first sight, is that each of these parts was written with a different set of words. But the reasoning was sound. The difference in meter between one text and another allowed rhythmic combinations that identical words would have made impossible under the system of musical notation then in use.

Adoption of the motet by secular composers brought more oddities. The love motet was the rage. Secular texts were linked with Gregorian teneur parts. A love song might be superimposed on a prayer to the Virgin Mary. French words were mounted on Latin texts. It was by no means unusual to hear a four-part motet combining a Gregorian teneur, a moral text, a love song and a hymn to Bacchus. In the end the Gregorian text was dropped altogether and replaced by an original secular text.

This mixture of the sacred and the secular was not as irreverent as it sounds, however. The notes of the liturgical teneur were, in fact, so long as to render the text unrecognizable. And in any case it was usually played on an instrument. It was merely a starting point, a vehicle. As for the combination of a number of texts in one composition, the great vocal quartets and quintets of opera employ the same device, and we see nothing objectionable in them.

Little by little, under the influence of lay society, the motet changed its character. It cast off its cloak of seriousness to reveal a suit of pungent wit and humor. It took society by storm—in particular, cultivated society. For as one theoretician, Jean de Grouchy, has explained, "This was not music for the common man, who could not understand its subtleties nor find pleasure in it. It was a music for the scholar, and for those who sought finesse in the arts."

The Conductus and the Tournai Mass

While the organum, having laid the foundations for the motet, was declining in importance through the 13th century, another form of composition, the

41

34 Procession with the Ark of the Covenant. The retinue includes a viellist, a harpist and a crowned figure playing a psaltery. (15th-century manuscript)
35 Organ being played by animals. The theme of animal musicians goes back to earliest times. There are examples in Sumer, in ancient Mesopotamia. (English—14th century)

35

conductus, was rising steadily, breaking free from the fetters of religious music.

Not that it abandoned the Church altogether. A number of examples exist in which the conductus interprets the mysteries of the liturgy. Jacques Chailley gives as an instance Perotinus' *Salvatoris hodie,* a "meditation on circumcision, in which the most precise details of the surgical operation were analyzed in terms of a mystic symbolism which might well offend modern prudery."

But the conductus did step beyond the confines of the Church and become one of the most favored vehicles of the traveling musicians of the goliard movement: the itinerant clerks, students, monks and former monks. The texts they used, usually in Latin, were often satirical or humorous and were frequently inspired by contemporary topics. The goliards sang them both in the taverns and in the abbeys where they spent the night, and this in no way inhibited their condemnations of the abuses of the Church or the follies of the monks. They even criticized the Pope.

Composition was extraordinarily free, even to 20th-century ears, and it employed not only the principle of imitation—the repetition by one voice of a musical phrase first used by another—but also that of invertible counterpoint, a device that permitted each voice to take either the duplum, tri-plum or quadruplum part without discordant consequences.

Another important point is that the polyphonic technique of the conductus, more than that of the motet, reveals an entirely new preoccupation with harmony.

Toward the end of the 13th century, for the first time, the polyphonic principles of the conductus were applied to liturgical composition. The result was the *Tournai Mass* in three voices. This was the first polyphonic Mass.

Although, as we have seen, the polyphonic forms of the Middle Ages were written for singers, there was never any question of their being sung by choirs. The concept of the choir is a modern one, dating only from the 18th century. The organum, the conductus, the motet, and the styles that followed them, the madrigal and the French *chanson,* were performed by soloists or by very small groups of singers. The voice in certain parts could be replaced by instruments, and from the 14th century on, numerous pieces could be performed by either singers or instruments.[16]

Adam de La Halle

If Adam de la Halle (*ca.* 1240-1285 or 1288) had merely been one of the scores of troubadours in

36

prosperous Arras, a city that maintained a particularly warm welcome for the jugglers, his name would be lost among those of his brother artists. If all we knew of his work was his songs, we would have no reason to single him out. But De La Halle —the Hunchback—was something else again.

Not that he stood aloof from the others. Like them, he took great delight in the long-drawn-out musico-literary debates of the *puys* (the troubadours' "courts of love"). There they would discuss such subjects as these: "If you were offered a beautiful mistress on condition that you carried her on your back to a rival, would you accept?" Or: "Would you give up peas if this sacrifice brought you affluence?" Or: "If you knew you were to enjoy the favors of your lady ten times in your life, would you make haste or delay this pleasure until later?"[17]

The Hunchback stands out by virtue of two works that belong to the history of literature even more than to music—the *Jeu de la Feuillée* (The Arbor) and the *Jeu de Robin et Marion* (The Story of Robin and Marion). Gustave Cohen, an authority on medieval romance literature, said of the *Jeu de la Feuillée* that it inaugurated French comic drama with a work that has more in common with Shakespearean fantasy than with Gallic farce.

The musical content of these two works is not of equal importance. De La Halle was content to adopt tunes from contemporary songs for his musical settings. The *Jeu de Robin et Marion* has frequently been compared with the *Devin du Village* (The Village Sorcerer) by Jean-Jacques Rousseau (1712-1778), and it has been called "the first French comic opera." But De La Halle, like the authors of the *Jeu de Daniel,* had no conscious desire to create a new form. His object was much simpler, to satisfy fashionable demand for *refrains*. The troubadours were already meeting the demand by quoting a favorite line of the audience at the end of each couplet of their songs. The romance poets, who may well have been responsible for the vogue, were doing it before the troubadours, punctuating their texts, which were generally read aloud, with quotations of popular refrains whose words and music they noted. A characteristic of these refrains is that, contrary to the normal modal language of the period, they favored the use of the major mode, and the minor mode was rarely used.

De La Halle's most original and personal contribution to the history of music consisted of his rondeaus. It is not merely the lively charm of their melody that draws attention. The Hunchback was the first to adapt the polyphonic technique of the

37

Latin conductus to the still monodic—for one voice—French rondeau, creating a new style.

The details of De La Halle's life, unlike those of Leoninus or Perotinus, are well known. He spent his youth in Arras, fell in love with a girl named Marie and married her. He spent some time studying in Paris and then returned to Arras, where he was supported by wealthy patrons. He took service with Robert II, Comte d'Artois and nephew of Louis IX, and accompanied him to Naples. He wrote the *Jeu de Robin et Marion* for the court of Charles, Comte d'Anjou, son of Louis VIII and conqueror of Sicily. (This court was still shaken by the bloody massacre of the French in Sicily in 1282, which was to provide the plot for Verdi's opera *The Sicilian Vespers,* six hundred years later.) Charles was evidently pleased with De La Halle's work, and the Hunchback probably spent the last years of his life, which ended prematurely at the age of forty-seven, in his service.

Change, contradiction and variety are the stuff of life, and the 13th century was no exception. This century of Louis IX, the king the French called St. Louis, is in some ways one of the peaks of Christianity. But this was also the century of Roger Bacon. From his scholarly eminence at Oxford, this ancestor of the modern scientist attacked the sacrosanct authority of the ancients and extolled the virtue of direct experiment and experience. His ever-watchful contemporaries saw the danger and threw him into prison, but there were other signs of a new era.

Feudalism was in decline. Trade was becoming ever more important. International banks and industry, heralds of capitalism, were coming into existence.[18]

Similar contrasts were to be found in the arts. On the one hand stood the purity of the Gothic cathedrals and the spiritual music of the school of Notre-Dame. On the other arose the rupture with Byzantine conventionalism, led by the sculptor Agostino di Duccio and the painter Giovanni Cimabue in Italy. In France there grew a more popularly based and more realistic culture, which replaced the *chanson de geste* with the *chantefable*—a mixture of recited prose and sung verse—and the narrative *chanson de toile,* and then the prose romance. It was an art that was to free itself progressively from the magico-musical element. At the same time, great poets were emerging from the ranks of troubadours and jugglers—men such as Dante in Italy and Rutebeuf in France.

Music, maturing slowly in the churches and in the abbeys, could not remain unaffected by all this and sought a new freedom. Contact with the world outside led to a relaxation of rigidity and

45

38

to the acceptance of an art of more popular origin. Instrumental music began to climb the ladder of social respectability, with the result that instruments began to gain a greater degree of individuality than ever before.

Ars Nova

The 14th century was not one of great inspiration in France. Certainly it cannot match the glory of Italy at that time. The late Gustave Cohen described the 14th century in France as "a continuation and a preparation," but he added, "it cannot stand alone." Although it is "incapable of exciting us," he said, "troubled as it was by external war and internal revolt, by the plague of 1348 and by the famine which was almost endemic, it does not, however, deserve either negligence or contempt."[19] There were no great painters, no writers of note in this, the century of Jacquerie—the peasant revolts—and the landing of English troops on French soil. Only one name stands out, that of a poet-musician, Guillaume de Machaut *(ca.* 1300-1377).

There was, of course, considerably more activity in music than this scarcity of genuine creative talent might suggest. But it was inspired by musicians whose theoretical and technical ingenuity took

precedence over poetic imagination and who expended their artistic energy more on pamphlets and manifestos than on durable works of music.

For this was an age of frequent and vehement disputes. For the first time we see a quarrel between the ancients and the modern—the guardians of tradition and the prophets of the music to come—spring up among musicians. Not for the last time did the defenders of *Ars Antiqua* (the art of the motet, on this occasion) heap scorn on "certain moderns" who had the effrontery to question the attainments of the past, while their opponents glowed with satisfaction at their own audacity.

The champion of the avant-garde, Philippe de Vitry (1291-1361)—court official, composer and Bishop of Meaux—coined the phrase *Ars Nova,* which was to become the password of the *novateurs.* Pope John XXII had already denounced the revolutionaries, but his decree, although it achieved a certain celebrity, was to prove totally ineffective.

Problems of Notation and Rhythm

The end of the 13th century and the 14th century brought decisive innovations in rhythmic notation, innovations of a subtlety sometimes remi-

39

40

niscent of the most recent researches of composers of the second half of the 20th century.

The need for a more exact rhythmic notation had been urgent ever since the time of Perotinus and the development of contrapuntal music. The most successful improvements came from two 13th-century experts, Franco de Colonia (Cologne) and Franco de Paris. With another Frenchman, Jean de Garlande, they were the principal theoreticians of mensural, or proportional music, which sought to soften the system of rhythmic modes, based on the Greek meters then in use for notation. In proportional music each note had a proper value. There were longs, breves and semibreves, but unlike our modern system, each of these was divided into three. One long was equal to three breves, one breve to three semibreves. For theological reasons—the Holy Trinity—music was always in triple time.

For many composers, the rule of triple time was a prison from which they sought to escape in order to write in any rhythm. It was De Vitry who was to unlock the door in 1325 with a treatise entitled *Ars Nova*.

This was a signal to composers to divide notes by two or by three as they saw fit, and to add first the minim, then the semiminim (crotchet) and the fusa (quaver) to increase the rhythmic possibili-ties. A quarter of a century earlier Pierre de La Croix had advocated dividing the breve into seven smaller values. Triple time became known as "perfect" time and was indicated by a circle at the beginning of the line. A semicircle indicated binary rhythm.[20]

Ars Nova brought a subtle and delicate development to the process of isorhythm, the periodic repetition of a rhythmic phrase.

"They cut melody into pieces with their hockets," complained John XXII in his papal letter denouncing the avant-garde. The hocket was another process much favored by the novateurs. It meant breaking melody into single notes or very short phrases by means of rests. Chailley described it well when he said that the hocket passages, while they break rhythm of the motet, give it a "slashed, abrupt character" that recalls the modern approach of Negro-American swing.

These various innovations were to lead composers into a frenzy of rhythmic subtlety on occasion, a tangle that presents unbelievably complex problems of notation to musicians attempting to transcribe these works for modern performance. It is hardly surprising, then, that so many 20th-century composers, from Stravinsky to Křenek, should have confessed to a keen interest in their work.

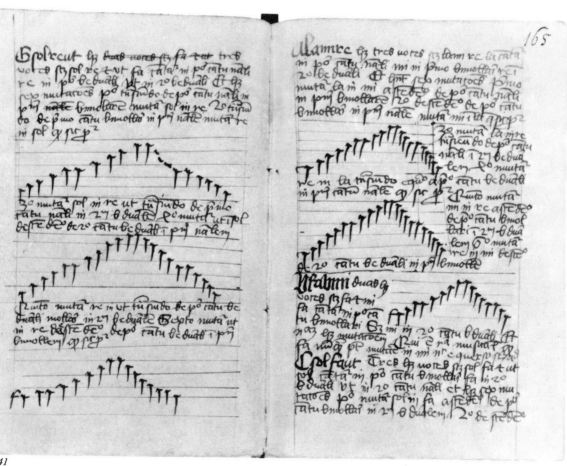

41

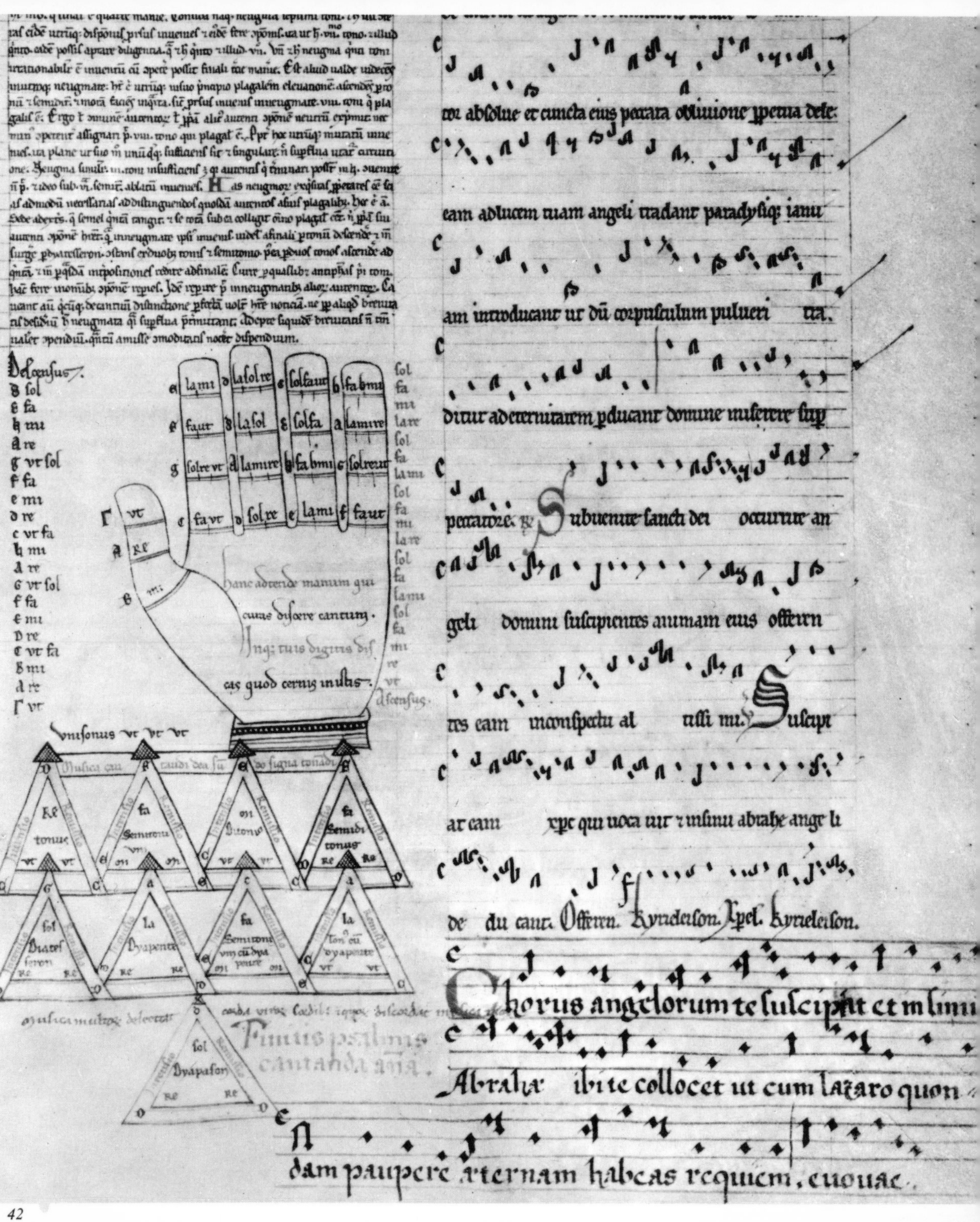
Descensus
Unisonus ut ut ut
Musica multos delectat
Chorus angelorum te suscipiat et in sinu
Abraha ibi te collocet ut cum lazaro quon
dam paupere aeternam habeas requiem. euouae

Oms̄ sc̄a discipli dn̄j. orā.
Sc̄e mauriti cū s. t. orā

Oms̄ sc̄i ꝺnnocentes orā
Sc̄e sebastiane orā

Sc̄e stephe orā
Sc̄e Thoma orā

Sc̄e Clemens orā
Sc̄e petre orā

Sc̄e corneli orā
Oms̄ sc̄a m̄res orā

Sc̄e cypane orā
Sc̄e siluester orā

Sc̄e laurenti orā
Sc̄e hylarij orā

Sc̄e vincenti orā
Sc̄e martine orā

tulas po tus muntus no tus ia nans re

bres ani me. ohſere Agnus. Cuius tach

tus re git actus voluit ſe au feras ſe ma

giſtro rum opti me. ohſe gn. di. O

uens au ra ſed ſetu ra vnge men tes te pe

ten tes fruc tus ſpe i maxi me. Do

etua uita. ch homo perpende fra

gilis mortalis et inſtabi lis qui vitare non pote

ris mortem quocumq; ieris. nam aufert te

ſepiſſime dum uiuis libentiſſi me anc

46 *Portrait of Guillaume De Machaut (1300?-1377), French poet and musician.*
47 *Illustration from a collection of poems by Guillaume De Machaut. De Machaut's musical works include ballads, virelais, rondeaus, lays, motets and the celebrated* Messe Notre-Dame, *the first polyphonic Mass in the history of music.*

46

De Vitry's view of musical composition found support from his friend, Johannes de Muris, and from Simon Tunsted in England and Marchetto in Italy. But Jacobus de Leodio, a Belgian theorist, remained faithful to the 13th century in his massive treatise *Speculum musicae,* written in seven books.

Guillaume De Machaut

Although in modern eyes Guillaume De Machaut (1300?-1377) is the only figure of artistic importance in the 14th century in France, other composers shared with him the favor of contemporary music lovers. Their names have come down to us, but no information about their works.

Until quite recently this was true even of Philippe de Vitry, De Machaut's only serious rival. Today we are able to attribute to this great theorist perhaps a dozen motets. They reveal an extraordinary ingenuity of composition, but it is generally agreed that they lack De Machaut's inspiration.

There is a curious parallel between the lives and personalities of De Machaut and Adam de La Halle. Both were poets and musicians, and, like the Hunchback, it was as a clerk and not as a musician that De Machaut was engaged by the King of Bohemia, Jean de Luxembourg.

For twenty years or so De Machaut accompanied his adventurous royal patron on his expeditions—from Paris and Luxembourg to Prague, from Italy to Poland, from Germany to Russia. But the king's blindness put an end to this restless, if invigorating life, and De Machaut returned to France to settle in Reims. He was in his forties and no doubt ready for a more peaceful existence. He was appointed a canon, and indulged his passion for hunting, perhaps reluctant to forget altogether the long journeys on horseback that had taken him all over Christendom.

When he was sixty, fifteen years before his death, a young girl of noble family from Armentières fell in love with him. They wrote to each other for three or four years, until the day the girl, Péronne, married. The affair caused a few raised eyebrows in the canon's household, but the correspondence survived, and it is all the more valuable to us because in his letters De Machaut talks frequently of his work and his compositions. There is no way of knowing what influence the love of this young girl had on his work, but it is known that a large number of his compositions were written during this period.

De Machaut enjoyed considerable respect for more than his worth as a musician. Witness not only his official functions for the Dauphin and the

47

Duc de Berry but also, and even more important, the number of diplomatic missions entrusted to him by the court of France.

His compositions include both secular and religious works: ballads, virelais, rondeaus, lays, motets and the famous *Messe Notre-Dame*—in all, nearly 150 musical works.

The ballad seems to have been his favorite vehicle. He wrote two hundred ballads, although he set only forty-two to music. One of these is for solo voice. He composed the instrumental teneur for the ballads himself, usually adopting a theme from the liturgical repertoire. Sometimes he added a second and a third instrument on top of the teneur. Thus his ballads are sometimes for a single voice accompanied by two instruments, or for two singers accompanied by two or three instruments.

But this man, who was a precursor in so many fields, was also the last to write virelais for solo voices. He called them "chansons balladées." All but five of his motets are secular. They reveal De Machaut as the first composer to add a contra-teneur to the teneur, an innovation that was to be rich with consequence, and to bring in the voices one after the other. His rondeaus frequently furnished him with a pretext for musical puns and for displays of his contrapuntal expertise.

The *Messe Notre-Dame* is still frequently, and incorrectly, known as the *Messe du Sacre de Charles V* (Mass for the Coronation of Charles V). It was not merely the first polyphonic Mass written by a single composer (the Tournai Mass was a combined effort), but also a masterpiece in its own right, as modern recordings reveal. In it, De Machaut gives free rein to his abundant creative talents. He achieves a marriage between the most extravagant innovations of Ars Nova and the science of Ars Antiqua. Evidence of his genius abounds in this rich, broad composition, a work that seems to combine the mysticism of the Middle Ages with their vigor and sometimes rugged candor.

De Machaut was a poet. And both in his poems and in the letters he wrote to Péronne he set down his ideas about his art—a valuable legacy for us now. One frequently quoted passage has these lines:

> For music is a cunning art
> Which bringeth laughter, song and dance
> Away, dull melancholy . . .
> Where'er she be she bringeth cheer,
> And charmeth all weighed down with care;
> Thus need we but to hear her voice
> She maketh every heart rejoice.

In another quotation, De Machaut had this to say about creative art:

> *He who hath not sentiment*
> *Makes mock with words and with his song.*

The poet's meaning is clear. He who writes poetry and music without soul creates nothing but caricature.

Among the anonymous works that have come down to us from the 14th century are a number based on bird song, on hunting and on battle. Several are worthy of note. Some of these works even are of sufficient caliber to rival the compositions on these themes written in the 16th century by Clement Janequin.[21]

We cannot leave 14th-century France without referring to the 132 compositions of different origin, motets and one-part works, that the compiler Chaillou de Pestain used to color the *Roman de Fauvel (ca.* 1312), a moralizing and allegorical verse romance by Gervais du Bus. It is through this collection that we have the ballads and rondeaus of Jean de Lescurel. They bear the hallmark of a great musician, both in the originality of their composition and in their inspiration. But De Lescurel, sadly, was to meet a premature death. He was hanged for rape and murder.

Italy in the 14th Century

During all this time, on the other side of the Alps, Italy was bursting with a fever of creation and giving the Renaissance its impetus. In all the arts the Italians were producing work that commands our admiration today. Primitive Sienese painting was at its height, with the talents of Duccio di Buoninsegna, Simone Martini and the brothers Pietro and Ambrogio Lorenzetti. In Florence Giotto was, in Leonardo da Vinci's phrase, "drawing what he sees" and establishing the foundations of an art that was to renew the pictorial vision of the entire West by setting out to conquer reality and life. (The painters were to discover the laws of perspective at the same time that the musicians were discovering the laws of classical harmony. Five centuries later they were to abandon these laws together.) Andrea Pisano cast the two bronze doors of one of the gates of the Baptistry. Another century was to pass before the others were entrusted to Ghiberti. The walls of the Campo Santo in Pisa were being covered with a gigantic and powerful fresco, the "Triumph of Death," worthy of the "Inferno" of the *Divine Comedy,* which Dante was just completing.

As Dante sang of his Beatrice, so Petrarch was celebrating his Laura. Boccaccio was writing the

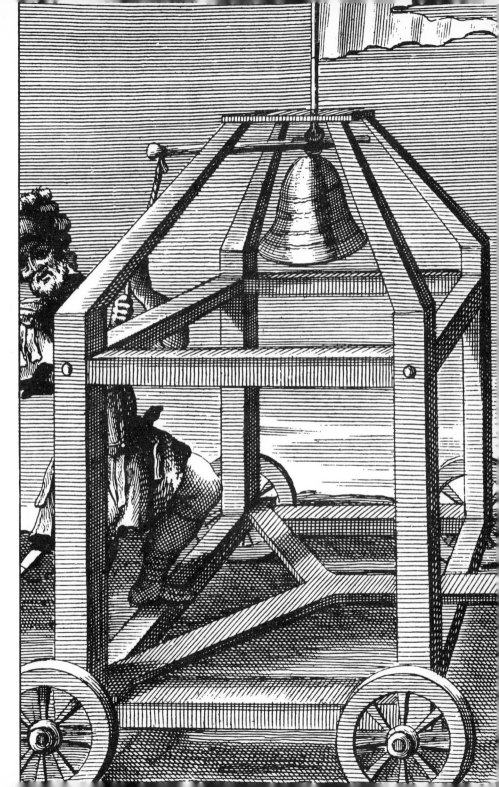

49 *Traveling bell.*
("Carroccio," taken
from Bonnani's
Gabinetto armonico, *1722)*

49

stories to which so many dramatists of later centuries were to turn for inspiration—the *Decameron.*

It was on the outskirts of Florence that Boccaccio placed the villa in which a group of young men and women, seeking escape from thoughts of the "black death," gathered to tell the racy stories that form so important a part of our literary heritage. And it was in Florence, under the influence of the French, that an Italian Ars Nova developed. It rapidly created its own quite original character.

The Italian composers made no effort to deny the parentage of this new music. Indeed, they frequently wrote their own settings to French words or introduced into their works quotations from De Machaut. Examples can be found in the work of Francesco Landino (1325-1397). Both De Machaut and De Vitry were greatly respected by the Italians. In addition to copying the work of the two Frenchmen, the Italians wholeheartedly adopted their techniques in the motet.

The Italian Ars Nova movement had its own theoretician, however—Marchetto de Padua. His two treatises, *Lucidarium in arte musicae planae* and *Pomerium artis musicae mensurabilis,* brought together and codified the aspirations of the Florentine musicians. Even more important, Marchetto's innovations in the field of notation were to lead to the final liberation of music from the fetters of the

et in lecula leculonum.

Amen.

Aue maria graaa ple
na dominus tecum

dauid xpm uenientē
nunaat jplm couocās.
enite exultemū
domino iubile

gnus d
magn
deos: q
rpellet
luam q
lunt o
et altit
ipe con
on
ue
mare e
andam
mani
dorem
ante de

...act erat in prin
cipio et nunc et semper
in secula seculorum.
amen. alleluya alla.
Enu crator ꝑ
spiritus men
tiorum uisita in
supena gratia que
tua sit pectora.
Demento salutis
tor quod nostri quod
in corporis ex illiba
uirgine nascendo
nam sumpsere.
Maria mater gratie
ter misericordie tu

ant. Brnitatu. ps. dd.

eatus uir qui
non abijt in
cnsilio impiorum

52

54

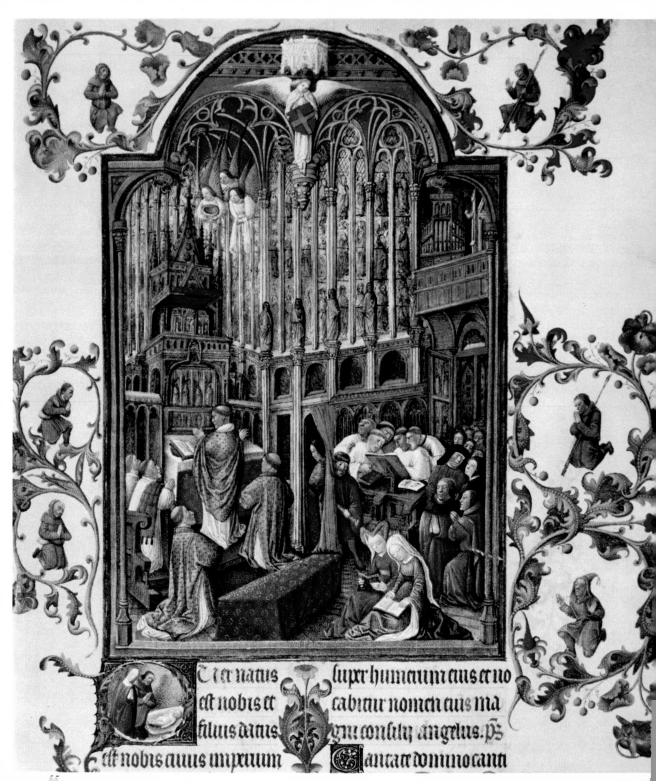

*55 Celebration of Mass as
depicted in this miniature from the
Très Riches Heures du Duc de Berry,
by Jean Colombe.*

text. Alfred Einstein dates the birth of polyphonic instrumental music from the publication of the *Pomerium* in 1309.

The most common form of composition employed by these musicians was the madrigal. But as with the motet, the 14th-century madrigal should not be confused with the five-voice Italian madrigal of the 16th century.

The creator of the madrigal—a style that is typically Italian—is thought to have been one Pietro Casella, a boyhood friend of Dante, who features in the poet's *Purgatory*. Unfortunately, none of Casella's compositions has survived.

The precise history of the word "madrigal" is uncertain. According to the historian Karl Nef, it was orginally a herdsman's song and later developed a kinship with the idyll, in its broadest sense, for the madrigal occasionally dealt with serious subject matter. It is usually short and light in treatment, with from six to thirteen lines and two or three rhymes. The texts are frequently taken from contemporary poets, Dante, Petrarch or Boccaccio. More often than not it is written for two voices. The melody is free and very ornate, while the bass, often instrumental, acts as a support. Compared with contemporary French composition, the madrigal is striking for its attractive melody and its charm.

The first masters of the Florentine madrigal were Giovanni da Cascia, an early 14th-century composer who was organist at the Cathedral of Santa Maria del Fiore and later moved to Verona, and Jacopo da Bologna in the middle years of the century.

Two other forms were popular among the Florentine composers: the *caccia* and the *ballata*. The caccia was aptly named. The word means a hunt, or a chase, and as a musical form it depends very much on a canon, which has several voices following each other with the same melodic phrase, rather like a huntsman pursuing his prey. Composers made extensive use of the hocket to add animation to the caccia. (The French term is *hoquet*. Literally translated, it means "hiccup," which gives some idea of the effect.) France had a similar form, the *chasse,* usually in three parts, but with the difference that while the chasse is purely a vocal form, the third voice in the caccia is instrumental. In both countries the term came to be used to describe any descriptive piece in canon form.

The ballata is no different in form from the French ballade, which is itself closely related to the virelai. Once a dancing song, it has three couplets followed by an envoi—a final stanza—which forms a refrain, or ritornello. As in the caccia, one voice is instrumental.

In all these forms, the Italians were to reveal a rich store of melodic invention, which led them to transfer the principal interest of the composition more and more from the teneur to the highest voice, the superius.

This development was accompanied by a move toward a liberal use of gay, light ornamentation in the superius. Initially, the ornamentation had been for instruments, but it was copied by singers to form the beginnings of *bel canto.* At the same time, the sensitivity of the Italian ear abolished sequences of fifths and octaves as too unpolished, opening the door for thirds and sixths.

Francesco Landino

Francesco Landino, or Landini, was born in Fiesole, some three miles outside Florence, in 1324. The most famous Italian composer of his age, he embodies the intensity of creative activity among the Florentine musicians of the second half of the 14th century.

"Everyone is writing madrigals, ballads, motets. Everyone regards himself as a second Vitry or a second Marchetto," wrote Jacopo da Bologna. "The world is so full of little masters, it is hard to find room for the disciples." The output of madrigals in particular was, by all accounts, immense.

Landino was the son of a painter. But he had very few years in which to enjoy the soft light of his native Tuscany or the view over Florence that his father knew so well. Still very young, Francesco contracted a pox that left him blind. Unable to use his eyes, he turned to music for fulfillment.

The broad outlines of his life have come down to us through the writings of a contemporary, Filippo Villani.

The young Francesco proved to have a considerable talent for music. His ability to master the most varied range of instruments was a constant source of wonder to his friends. Within a very short time he was expert at the lute, the guitar, the flute and the keyboard instruments, particularly the organ. He was appointed organist at the church of San Lorenzo in Florence, and from there his fame spread rapidly far beyond the borders of Tuscany —fame as a poet and as a composer as well as a musician. He became one of the most honored musicians of the time and was publicly crowned with laurels in Venice by Pierre Lusignan, King of Cyprus.

If we are to believe one contemporary writer, Giovanni da Prato, even the birds recognized the quality of Landino's art. Da Prato describes how the birds stopped singing, so great was their delight, on one occasion when Landino was playing

the portative organ in a garden. Then a nightingale settled on the tree beneath which the blind organist was seated, and the two engaged in a contest of virtuosity.

Nearly one hundred fifty of Landino's compositions have come down to the present day. They have a range of melody and a depth and sweetness of expression that set him far above his contemporaries.

Indeed, he was far above his successors. They proved skillful in imitating the French and Flemish composers, but brought no originality to their music. Not until the 16th century and the time of Giovanni da Palestrina do we find a figure equal to Landino south of the Alps.

John Dunstable

Surprisingly, perhaps, for her literature is one of the richest and most entertaining in Europe, England holds no important place in the history of music. Her poets have always shown themselves more truly musicians than her composers, and her music has produced no one of the stature of a Shakespeare for inspirational power and genius.

Until the 15th century, English music in general is little more than an adjunct of the French. Its originality lies in its moderated application of Continental innovations, which it embraces without renouncing its own special harmonic style. It is a style, notable for its full, rich sonority, that grew out of the English use of the third (a legacy of the two-part singing of the *gymel,* with its parallel thirds) and even of the sixth (as in the three-part harmonization of the fauxbourdon). French theorists were still reluctant to give their blessing to such intervals.

For a long time the canon was thought to be an English development, a belief based on a delightful double canon, *Sumer is icumen in* (Summer is coming in), which was thought to have been written in 1240. There is now evidence, however, that it dates from no earlier than 1300.

In spite of the paucity of her musical invention, England was not without a part to play. For it was the English who were to conduct the transition from the Franco-Italian Ars Nova in its dying moments to the great epoch of Franco-Flemish music. At no other time was English influence on the music of Europe quite so rich—thanks, to some extent, to the political situation. For the French defeat at Agincourt brought about a complete reversal in Anglo-French relations.

Much as the Norman conquest encouraged the attraction for English musicians and scientists of the innovations brought in by the school of Notre-

73

58

Dame and the teachings of the University of Paris, so the advance of English troops onto Continental soil and their occupation of a large part of France was to give effective support to the spread

59

58 *The tombstone of Francesco Landino (1324?-1397), the renowned blind composer, lutist and organist from Florence. (Basilica of San Lorenzo, Florence—14th century)*
59 *Musician holding a bowed instrument, probably of the rebec type. (late 15-century woodcut)*
60 *Winged demon beating a drum.*

of art forms from the English side of the Channel. For it was not merely English music that grew in influence; the "flamboyant" English version of Gothic architecture began to appear in France, too.

The outstanding figure of the time in English music was John Dunstable (*ca.* 1370-1453), an astronomer as well as a composer. The details of his life are obscure, but he appears to have spent some time in Italy and France. He was attached to the retinue of the Duke of Bedford, which would support at least the thesis that he visited France. For the duke was Regent of France until Charles VI came of age, and he lived for a long time in Paris, where he maintained a chapel. Thomas Hoppinel, one of the leaders of the Notre-Dame choir school, was a member of the chapel.

Dunstable's considerable renown is indicated by the inscription in Latin on his tomb at the church of St. Stephen Walbrook in London. It reads: "This man, O music, was your prince, your glory, your light, who spread the beauty of your art across the world." His name was indeed known throughout Europe. Much of his fame was due to the widely read writings of the Flemish theoretician Johannes Tinctoris (who died in 1511).

Some fifty works by Dunstable have been preserved, and all, with the exception of three songs, come within the framework of sacred music. I

them he achieves a harmonious marriage of English tradition with French and Italian influence. They are simple and natural, the result of Dunstable's efforts to avoid the excesses and distortion of Ars Nova. His melody is gentle and smooth, after the example of the Florentines.

The importance of Dunstable's contribution to music, however, lies primarily in the novelty of his rich harmonic conception. The teneur finally loses its role of principal support to the superior voice. And although the writing is contrapuntal, one frequently feels it was conceived vertically. He takes care to soften any harshness caused by friction between the voices or by syncopation by a sparing use of devices such as suspension or retardation. In this way he creates a constant feeling of euphony that his contemporaries found striking.

Dunstable was something of an architect in sound, and here again he was an innovator. In order to create a stronger unity he linked the five parts of the Ordinary of the Mass with identical musical material, either the same canto fermo as a foundation or the same initial motif.

His work also displays great skill in the art of varying the different stanzas of liturgical melody.

Other composers of talent—though of less importance—moved in Dunstable's circle. The principal one was Leonel Power, who died in 1445.

61   *The wedding of Boccaccio Adimari
and Lisa Ricasoli.
Reed-pipes and trumpet.
Only the nobility and the upper middle
class had the right to be married
to the sound of trumpets.
(detail from a 15th-century Florentine
painting, artist unknown)*

62   *Sea monster holding a lute. The influence of Jerome Bosch is plain
in this detail from the painting by Jan Mandy (1500-1560).*

The 15th Century — an End and a Beginning

There are a number of ways of looking at the 15th century, this age that received its musical impetus from the English school of Dunstable. The humanists of the 16th century regarded it as the end of the Middle Ages. Certain German and American historians, on the other hand, see it as the real beginning of the Renaissance.

In fact, the 15th century was not a dividing line at all in any realistic sense.

In music, the polyphony of the Franco-Flemish school is the rich and natural development of the counterpoint of preceding centuries. It is less an innovation than a fulfillment. Even Josquin des Prés (*ca.* 1450-1521), whose genius enriched both the dying 15th century and the emergent 16th, belongs no more to one than to the other. He is a point of arrival as well as of departure. His work, like that of Johann Sebastian Bach, who found himself in a situation historically comparable in many respects, looks at one and the same time to the past and to the future.

The passage from one to the other, however, is achieved without upheaval, without any brutal turn-about, and so calmly as to be almost imperceptible.

In short, as Gustave Cohen has said, for the idea

of a rupture between two ages that men such as Erasmus and Rabelais, Du Bellay and Ronsard so strongly defended, "it would be better to substitute that of continuity and renewal by external contributions and internal evolution."[22]

The striking feature of the 15th century is its profound duality. It is an age of contrast and pathos. There are hired mourners at the tombs of the "sumptuous dead," but in the *Grands Mystères de la Passion* the emphasis is entirely human, on the sufferings at Calvary and the anguish of the Virgin.

This is the age of Joan of Arc, but also of Gilles de Retz, the original Bluebeard; of the wildness of François Villon and the sensitivity of Charles d'Orléans. It is the century that produced the paintings of Jan Van Eyck, Nicholas Froment, Maître de Moulins, Roger Van der Weyden, master of pathos, Hans Memling and Hugo Van der Goes, and the sculpture of Claus Sluter—all artists whose religious feeling and mysticism of the purest kind are allied to the objectivity of an unsurpassed realism. Not for an instant does the strictest discipline of precision destroy in them human tenderness and emotion. Yet it was also the century that produced the disturbing pictorial fantasies of Jerome Bosch.

The common people endured extreme misery and suffering (the Hundred Years' War was to end only in 1453) while the court of Burgundy lived in extravagant luxury and the towns of Flanders amassed great wealth. Asceticism and high religious principle were contrasted with a dissolute clergy and a lascivious brotherhood of monks.

But to return to music, and particularly to what the old textbooks called the Dutch school. Today it is more usual to call it the Franco-Flemish school, but it would be more precise, perhaps, to call it the Hainaut school. For it is a curious fact that nearly all the composers of any importance in this century were natives of this Franco-Belgian area between Brabant and Picardy.

Like Artois, Flanders, Holland, northern France and later Luxembourg, Hainaut formed part of the powerful Duchy of Burgundy, whose role—political and artistic—was to be considerable in the middle years of the century.

The whole area from the lower Rhine to the Somme was, at that time, one of the richest in Christendom. Bruges, one of the most important trading centers, could rival Genoa and Venice in volume of business. The affluence of the bourgeoisie had given them a taste for the arts, although certainly other circumstances helped inspire in 15th-century Flanders one of the finest schools of painting Europe has ever produced. A movement of this size cannot grow unless it coincides with the

63

64 Actors and jugglers entertaining
the court, with musicians playing the bass
bombard in the gallery. One of the
jugglers is holding a set of bagpipes.
(Chronique d'Angleterre—15th-century)
65 Detail from "The Last Judgment"
by Jerome Bosch. The gruesome striker
of the bell is a human body.

65

interests of its public, responds to a need and fulfills a demand. For art can only aspire to complete fulfillment if it obeys a need of what Jules Romains would have called the "unanimous soul." Otherwise it is nothing more than a vain game of aesthetics.

As with painting, a feeling for music was deeply rooted in the Flemish people. They were accustomed to music in the gatherings of society.[23] Lodovico Giucciardini wrote in 1588 of the inhabitants of Flanders:

"They are the true masters of musical art, which they have restored and brought to the highest level of perfection. For it is so natural to them, and indeed one might say innate, that men and women sing naturally in time, with the greatest grace and harmony; and as they have added artistic culture to these natural gifts, so they have raised themselves to this talent for instrumental and vocal music we see displayed every day and which, rightly, has taken them into all the courts of the Christian princes."

The dukes of Burgundy had not only a sense of grandeur and the broadest political ambitions. They had, too, a taste for books and prints, for sumptuous and brilliant banquets, for music and for the arts. Philippe the Good, Duke of Burgundy from 1419 to 1467, thought as highly of the character of Van Eyck as of his talents and fre-

quently entrusted him with secret missions. The artists of Flanders—painters, poets and musicians —found the dukes invaluable patrons.

After the acquisition of Flanders and the Netherlands, Burgundy became an industrial and maritime power, a mixed Germano-Latin state. By midcentury it was one of the great centers of European civilization. Musicians found at court patrons who were well informed about music and a highly select group of colleagues who ranked among the finest artists in the world.

The Chapel of the Dukes of Burgundy

The 15th century saw the noblemen beginning to assemble in their courts groups of musicians to form chapels—not, however, the same thing as orchestras, a concept that was still a long way off. Johannes Tinctoris gives this description of them:

"Very Christian princes . . . in order to bring magnificence to Divine Service and following the example of David, have established chapels, where they maintain at great expense different singers to praise God in a manner which is both pleasant and worthy of Him, with different voices raised in harmony. And since the princes' singers gather unto themselves honor, glory and riches, many have

83

embraced this profession with zeal. This is why music has made in this time such marvellous progress that it has seemed like the birth of a new art."

At first, then, the chapels brought together groups of singers. Before long they were joined by instrumentalists, although it was not until the 18th century that the instrumentalists began to take precedence.

The importance of the chapels is plain. In the words of Karl Nef, "These institutions now became the most remarkable repositories of musical art, and were to remain so for several centuries."

The chapel of the dukes of Burgundy was renowned for its quality. Philippe is known to have been extremely selective in his choice of musicians, minstrels or singers.

At the time of Philippe's son, Charles the Bold, who succeeded to the duchy in 1467, the Burgundy chapel consisted of twenty-four singers, child choristers, an organist, a guitarist and several viol and oboe players.[24] Molinet, historian of the court of Burgundy, left this description:

"And as King Charlemagne honored this science in his time when he summoned expert musicians from Rome to instruct those of France in true modulation, so Duke Charles received the most famous singers in the world and maintained a chapel filled with voices of such harmony and de-

66

84

light that there was no greater joy before the glory of Heaven."

According to Cartellieri, the singers of the Burgundy court were the objects of special favor. Like the heralds, they received raw meat at table.

The love of music was shared by such figures as King Charles V and King Charles VI of France, the Dukes of Berry, Guyenne and Touraine, and many others. All exercised great care in selecting their organists, their singers and their minstrels. In 1501, at the court of Philippe the Fair, Archduke of Austria, King of Castille and Prince of the Netherlands, there were, indeed, two ensembles— a "Grande Chapelle" and a "Petite Chapelle." Between them they counted thirty-nine performers, excluding the child choristers.[25]

Music and the "Entremet"

What was the role of the chapels? At the court of Burgundy, from 1431, by decree of Philippe the Good, they were required to perform a Mass daily. According to Cartellieri, Philippe's son, Charles, took a lively pleasure in the performance of the Mass, but "also enjoyed music outside Divine Service."

Philippe, who is said to have played the harp, appears to have given his son a particularly strong

67

68

69

72

musical education. Charles, as a child, received lessons in counterpoint from Robert Morton, an excellent composer of the Dunstable school. (Morton was one of a number of Englishmen who served at the Burgundy court, and it was, in fact, through them that the Franco-Flemish musicians knew about the ideas of Dunstable and his group.)

Charles, who had his own harp from the age of seven, composed several "well-constructed and well-written songs" and a motet that was sung in the church at Cambrai.[26] He suffered frequent attacks of melancholy, from which, it is reported, he sought cure and consolation in music. When his favorite painter, Hugo Van der Goes—a hypersensitive, self-doubting personality—sank into a state of depression that came close to insanity, Charles commanded that music be played frequently in the artist's presence, in memory of the sufferings of King Saul. Molinet wrote that music was "the resonance of the heavens, the voice of the angels, the joy of Paradise, the hope of the air, the organ of the Church, the song of small birds, *the relaxation of all saddened and woeful hearts, the persecution and the harassment of devils, as is shown by David playing his harp before King Saul, who was possessed by demons.*"[27] This reveals that the 15th century had not forgotten the therapeutic role the ancients attributed to music.

Outside of religious services, the principal function of the chapel was to play at table and to embellish with music the famous *entremet,* which was so highly developed at the court of Burgundy. The modern meaning of the word is a sweet, or dessert, but the 15th-century connotation was rather different. It referred to the entertainments— a mixture of pantomime, tableau, dancing and music—performed to amuse the guests between dishes.

The decorative and visual, and indeed mechanical and architectural, element of the entremet was of a very high standard. In addition to musicians, the dukes maintained a small army of painters, decorators and poets whose task was to conceive and to create the subjects of the entremet on the occasion of a major festival. For the most important celebrations, highly placed lords and the most influential counselors were consulted. The entire Western world looked with admiration on this court, which seemed so determined to rival the courts of the Italian Renaissance. Festival succeeded festival, no two alike. And from near and far knights, lords and aristocrats from England, Germany, Italy and Spain traveled to Burgundy with the peers of France.

At the famous *Fêtes du Faisan* (Festival of the Pheasant), Cartellieri says, certain guests of

89

noble origin "came from very far away, undismayed even by sea voyages," to watch the entremet in disguise from the top of a platform, without taking part in the banquet. "One also saw certain bourgeois," he says.

Some entremets illustrated proverbs; others took their themes from mythology. Music played an active role, as the following examples show. They come from the Fêtes du Faisan, which Philippe the Good intended as a prelude to a new crusade to deliver Constantinople from the hands of the infidel.

At one end of the duke's table, among other sets, a church had been constructed, complete with belltower and stained glass windows. In it were four musicians to "entertain with songs and organ music." On a rock the naked figure of a small boy sprayed rose-water in the most natural of fashions. On another table, twenty-eight musicians sat in a giant pie.

"When the noise made by the guests had begun to die down a little, the church bell . . . began to make itself heard distinctly. The musicians in the church alternated with those in the pie. Beside the singers, who rendered, among others, the chanson *Saulvegarde de ma vie* (Safeguard of my life) and a motet, and together with them, all kinds of instruments were played."

Numerous interludes were presented, under the direction of sixteen gentlemen in ducal costume.

"First, there was a performing horse. In a cloth of red silk it entered the room backwards and walked around in the same manner. On its back were mounted two trumpeters, without a saddle and back to back. They wore gray and black tunics and surprising hats. Their faces were hidden by masks. A monster in white and green silk, its upper part man, its lower part griffon, rode astride a boar, also decked in green silk. He juggled with two daggers and a sword and carried on his shoulders an acrobat standing on his hands with his feet in the air. A beautiful white stag with gilded antlers entered. On its cloth of red silk sat a boy of twelve, in a short costume of crimson silk, a little black hat and shoes of pony skin. The child sang in a clear voice the chanson *Je ne vis oncques la pareille* (I never saw the like), accompanied only by the white stag, which was artificial. A dragon spouting fire flew across the room, then mysteriously disappeared."[28]

These frenetic scenes might have come from a surrealist mind centuries later.

A last example is taken from the celebrations for the third marriage of Charles the Bold, to Margaret of York, sister of the king of England,

74

in Bruges. The following entremet closed the grand banquet:

"Giants brought in a whale, sixty feet long and higher than a man on horseback. The animal could move its fins, its body and its tail; its eyes were fashioned from big mirrors which had been made movable. When the whale, to a great blowing of trumpets, arrived before the duke, it opened its jaws and out sprang two sirens. They sang a striking chanson, then performed a moresque dance with sailors who had leapt from the animal behind them. But jealousy and argument were not long in coming between them; the men beat each other until the giants made them return inside the whale with the sirens."[29]

Among the artists who took part in the production of these entremets were the composers Gilles Binchois (*ca.* 1400-1460) and Antoine Busnois (died 1492) and the painters Hugo Van der Goes and Jacques Daret, a pupil of Robert Campin. At the court of the Sforzas in Milan in the next century the great organizer of celebrations was, for a time, Leonardo da Vinci.

The use of artists of this stature was understandable. Apart from the tournaments, which were more in the nature of sporting contests, festivals and celebrations enlivened with music and acrobatics were the only entertainment of the great. Neither opera nor ballet, which were later to answer the need, incorporating imagination and the taste for show and complex machinery into scores and durable works, existed then. Even the theatre existed in little more than the mystery plays, and they were performed only rarely.

With this in mind, it is easier to assess the important position the musicians held at court and the role they had to play. Essentially—and this was true whether they wrote for the Church or for the laity—their work was written with a specific occasion in mind.

Forms: The Chanson

The 15th century has been called the golden age of the French *chanson*. And certainly it was a form that everyone took up merrily. Its popularity was such that writers were hard pressed to satisfy demand. Throughout the century copyists filled their manuscripts with chansons, to such an extent that more than a hundred *chansonniers* are known to us today. It was a type of song that everyone sang everywhere, in the towns as in the castles. It was part of the entertainment in the Burgundy entremets, as we have just seen. Charles d'Orléans had both words and music of the chanson *Madame, je suis plus joyeux* (Madame, I am more joyful)

91

75

embroidered on his sleeves, a fashion promptly adopted by the court of Ferrara. In palaces at Mantua and at Urbino, chansons were worked into the marquetry.

It even reached into the torture chamber: Witness the condemned man who cheerfully hummed, as he handed himself over to his executioners, "Ho drink, you have brought me death . . ."[30]

All over Europe people transcribed French chansons, often on magnificently illustrated manuscripts, for various instruments—the organ, the spinet, and particularly the lute, which the Christians had adopted from the infidels and which was now all the rage.

The cult of the chanson coincided with the decline of the ballad, which was going out of fashion. The initial impetus seems to have come from England. France, occupied by the English, had good reason to be familiar with their music, and Dunstable himself, remember, spent some time in Paris.

It was the melodic character of the invaders' music that captured the French. Composers sought to copy the English. Like them—though the English, on this point, were themselves copying the Italians—they began to set the melody in the highest voice, the superius, instead of in the tenor. (The Italian term was slowly replacing the French *teneur*.) It was this modification, indeed, that made the essential difference between the new style and traditional composition.

As a rule, 15-century chansons were written for three or four voices. They were performed sometimes *a cappella* (entirely without accompaniment) and sometimes backed by instruments. There were three preferred styles, the rondeau, the bergerette and the virelai. The subjects varied considerably, but love was the most frequent. And it was love in all its forms, from the courtly to the erotic, from lament to pique.

The poets made frequent use of the acrostic to air their grievances or to take their revenge on a girl who had deceived them. It could be a sharp kind of vengeance, too, if defamatory on occasion. The poets were by no means afraid of a four-letter word!

Only the political chanson had disappeared, victim of a police decree in 1395. Minstrels who referred to the Pope, the king or the nobles of France in their songs made themselves liable to a fine or a prison sentence.

The old minstrel, incidentally, the poet-composer, was by now a figure of the past. No longer were musicians their own "librettists."

But in all its forms, the French chanson at this time enjoyed a truly international popularity.

92

77 Chapel performing a vocal religious work, with the score placed on a lectern. From the 15th century the courts as well as the churches maintained chapels, restricted initially to singers but later including instrumentalists.
(early 16th-century French manuscript)
78 Portrait of Guillaume Dufay, one of the great masters of the 15th century, and Gilles Binchois, whose chansons earned him the nickname "Father of joyousness."

Many a composer needing a canto fermo for a Mass was to seek inspiration from this copious source.

The Motet and the Mass

While the chanson was winning this immense popularity, the motet began to look back to its origins, turning away from the world of lay music and toward the Church. It abandoned the principle of isorhythm. It forgot the habit of superimposing different texts. Henceforth all the voices were to sing identical words. There were three or four parts, certain ones of which could be played on instruments. In a four-part motet, the tenor lost its primary role to the superius.

Despite the extent of the demand for the chanson, it is another example of the fundamental character of contrast of the 15th century that it was also an age of marked resurgence in religious music. As the century progressed, indeed, there was a clear shift of emphasis from lay music to the music of the Church. In the time of Josquin des Prés, the Mass was to rise and become the pinnacle of artistic endeavor.

If we consider the development of Franco-Flemish music in its historical and spiritual context, this is not really surprising. From the middle of the 14th century, the Rhineland and Flanders witnessed a prodigious explosion of mysticism, with such figures as Johann Eckhart in Germany, Jan Van Ruysbroek in Flanders, and Johannes Tauler in Alsace. Gustave Cohen, whose studies of the Middle Ages make him an invaluable source of reference, saw clearly that it was this northern mysticism that provided the inspiration for the Franco-Flemish naturalist school of Van Eyck, Froment, Sluter and Van der Weyden. There were others, too. The primitives of the Rhineland with their blue madonnas seated in rose arbors spring from the same source, in their own innocent and ethereal way. Matthias Grünewald (ca. 1465-1528), the magnificent German painter, continued the trend into the 16th century. Karl Huysmans, in his unique assessment of the altarpiece of Issenheim, expressed the pathos and the dualism of the 15th century when he described Grünewald as the "most frantic of the realists" and the "most frantic of the idealists."[31]

This same mysticism inspired in the north a religious movement whose adherents called themselves the "Brothers of the Common Life." It was they who provided the first inspiration for such an exalted figure as the Dutch scholar Desiderius Erasmus. Their object was to fight the ungodliness of the laity and the laxity of the clergy. The

Brothers observed strict rules of humility and poverty, and their ideal of piety had a wide impact, particularly in the Netherlands and southern Germany. Not unnaturally, their activities aroused the mistrust of the Church, but the movement was nevertheless approved by the Council of Constance in 1415. One of its defenders was Pierre d'Ailly, Bishop of Cambrai. His cathedral was one of the principal centers of the religious music of the Franco-Flemish school.[32]

Whether or not the composers we are to discuss were in personal contact with the Brothers of the Common Life is unimportant. For the most part, an artist expresses the profound movements of his age unconsciously. He is the seismograph of history, of the obscure tremors and the mysterious upheavals of its hidden layers.

Technically, the 15th-century Mass followed the lead given by Dunstable, strengthening its internal structure and establishing its unity. Starting with the Flemish composer Guillaume Dufay (died 1474), the five parts of the Mass used a single theme to act as a link between them. Sometimes each part appears as a variation on the theme. Sometimes the theme itself is divided into a number of elements, each of which is freely used in different parts of the work. The origin of the theme is clear from the title.

But this canto fermo is not necessarily a liturgical theme. Its roots frequently lie in a chanson. Hence the *Homme armé* (the Armed Man) gave his name to several Masses. Others had titles such as *Se la face ay pale* (If the face is pale) or *À l'ombre d'un buissonet* (In the shade of a bush). Needless to say, the themes from these chansons, written in lengthened values, reversed and modified, were unrecognizable. Their purpose was purely architectural, simply to assure the unity of the work.

A composer could also build his Mass around a short motif of a few notes, without any reference to a text. It then became known as a *Missa supra voces musicales*. If the parts of the Mass were not linked by any kind of canto fermo, it was a *Missa sine nomine*. Yet another approach for the composer was to bring into play elements used by himself or by another composer whom he sought to honor—in a motet, perhaps. This is the device of parody, and a Mass of this type is known as a parody Mass. (The habit of enriching an existing composition by the addition of one or more voices was common at the time. And one of the voices added in this way could, in its turn, act as the tenor for a further work by a third composer.)

Imitation was another process utilized by the composers of the 15th century, and they exer-

79   Angel playing vièle à roue,
a kind of hurdy-gurdy,
as depicted in one of the "Heures,"
or Book of Hours, a form of
prayer book containing the different
orders of Divine Service. The "Petites
Heures" contained forms not included
in the main services. They were
often illustrated by leading artists.
(Heures de la Duchesse de Milan—
15th century—British Museum)
80   Angel playing the drum and the flute.
(Heures de la Duchesse de Milan)

80

cised a masterly skill in its development. They were, equally, virtuosos of the canon in all its forms—whether by inversion, by augmentation or by diminution.

The Composers: Binchois

Gilles de Binche (1400?-1460), known as Binchois, was born in Mons, Belgium. He served as a soldier until the Duke of Suffolk, on his way through Paris, recognized his musical talent and took him into his service.

It is to the duke, in all probability, that Binchois owed his poetic taste. For Suffolk, who had married the granddaughter of Chaucer, was a poet himself and wrote verse both in English and in French. He had friendly ties with Charles d'Orléans, whose verse Binchois frequently set to music. In the same way, he often took inspiration from the work of Christine de Pisan and Alain Chartier, displaying a perception rarely found among the chanson composers.

Binchois later took holy orders, and from 1430 he served at the court of Burgundy as chaplain to Philippe the Good. He remained there until his death, thirty years later, and he took part in the preparation of the court entertainments.

Binchois wrote both chansons and religious music, but it was the former that brought him the greatest celebrity. The forty or so chansons he left to posterity have a pleasing, natural simplicity. They are written for three voices, with words for the superius alone. The tenor and the counter-tenor were, therefore, probably intended for instruments. The subject of his chansons is usually courtly love. Little variation is evident in the manner of their composition, which shows no development, but it is undoubtedly this area of his work that brought him the nickname "Father of joyousness."

The religious music of the soldier-turned-priest is less consistent and not of comparable merit. In terms of quantity, too, it is less significant. The technique is traditional, and although Binchois was a friend of Guillaume Dufay, he failed to subscribe to his innovations.

None of his Masses employs the cyclic device of the unifying theme. He is content to carry over the florid language of his chansons. His works of a hymnal character—the Magnificat, the Gloria, the Te Deum, the Psalm—are notable for a fairly primitive use of the fauxbourdon; and although his motets reveal more subtlety, they remain faithful to the isorhythmic composition of Ars Nova.

81

Essentially, what Binchois sought in his music was the grace of the lyrical cantilena and flexibility in melody. His inspiration has much freshness and a touch of gentle melancholy, but he never achieved true greatness.

Guillaume Dufay

Guillaume Dufay (1400?-1474) was a contemporary of Binchois, but a musician of a quite different caliber. His life was as unsettled and vagabond as Binchois' was sedentary.

He is believed to have been born in Cambrai, France, where he made early contact with music as a chorister in the cathedral school. He went to Italy as a youth and was in the service of the Malatesta family in Rimini. He was later in France again but returned to Italy to the court of Ferrara.

In 1428 he became cantor to Pope Martin V. Between 1434 and 1437 he divided his time between the papal court and that of his protector, Amédée VIII of Savoy—the antipope Felix V! In about 1440 he was back in Cambrai as a canon, but between 1453 and 1458 he returned to the court of Savoy. He bore the title of chaplain to the court of Burgundy, but he could not have spent much time there. He returned to Cambrai before his death on November 27, 1474.

The Angel Musicians

81 *Angel playing the bowed vielle.*
(Heures de la Duchesse de Milan)
82 *Child angels playing various instruments:*
the trumpet, the drum, the triangle, the bellows flute.
Detail from an altarpiece by Jakob Cornelise van
Oostsanen, known as Jacob of Amsterdam (1470-1533?).
(Kassel Museum, West Germany)
83 *St. Cecilia playing the portative organ.*
Detail from a painting on wood by an unidentified
artist known only as the Master of the altarpiece
of St. Bartholomew. The portative organ could be
played by one person, one of the hands operating a
small bellows and the other working the keyboard.
(Cologne—late 15th century)
84 *Saint playing the psaltery. Detail from the*
"Virgin and Child" by Turino Vanni. Note that the
musician is holding a plectrum in each hand.
(Louvre, Paris)
85 *Angel playing the mandola, or mandora,*
a kind of small lute that is accepted as the
forerunner of the mandolin, which is first mentioned
in the 15th century. The mandola was played until
the 19th century, although it had been relegated to
the rank of a folk instrument by then. Detail from
the "Virgin and Child" by Sassetta. (Louvre, Paris)
86 *Angel playing the vielle. Detail from the*
"Virgin and Child" by Vanni.
87 *Angel holding a tambourine. Detail from*
the "Virgin and Child" by Sano di Pietro (1406-1481).
The tambourine, which enables a dancer to accompany
himself as he dances, enjoyed great popularity
among the peoples of southern Europe. At the same
time, however, it has always been associated
with other instruments, and has been included
in the modern symphony orchestra. (Museum of Art, Siena)
88 *Angel playing a* vièle à roue, *occasionally*
called a chifonie. Detail from the same work.
89-92 *Four angels playing the reed-pipe,*
the vielle, the trumpet and the tambourine.
(Fra Angelico—Les Offices, Florence)

98

89

90

91   92

93

108

His travels brought him into contact with the musical élite in France and, particularly, in Italy. In art it was the age of Fra Angelico, of Filippo Lippi, of Donatello and Verrocchio. Brunelleschi had completed the cupola of the Cathedral of Santa Maria del Fiore in Florence, and Dufay was commissioned to write two motets—*Nuper rosarum flores* and *Terribilis est locus iste*—for the solemn dedication of the dome on March 25, 1436. The following year he was in Bologna, and he also appears to have visited Naples.

94

Dufay's works include both religious and secular music. His chansons are notable for their spontaneity of movement, the pure elegance of their melodic line, and what the French musicologist André Pirro called their "happy blend of vigor and abandon."

Dufay was a master of the short composition and also of the wider form of the Mass. We have already seen the role he played in the development of the cyclic Mass, a style he pursued particularly in the second half of his career. The *Homme armé,* the *Ecce ancilla Domini* and the *Ave Regina Coelorum* are probably the finest examples from this portion of his work. His hymns have remained famous, and for good reason.

His work with the motet can be divided into two sections. The first group are isorhythmic, but

95

Dufay sought to imbue them with a new spirit. The others have been defined by the Swiss authority Jacques Handschin as motet-cantilenas. They reveal the influence of the Belgian composer and theorist Johannes Ciconia, canon of Padua in the late 14th century, and they are marked by Dufay's abandonment of the rhythmic complication of Ars Nova.

Briefly, Dufay's historical importance lies in his ability to clarify the heritage of the past and to put forward new solutions, particularly in the Mass, where he can be seen as Dunstable's spiritual heir.

"Dufay was perhaps the first to perfect poly-melodic writing, in which harmony and counterpoint are evenly balanced and neither is dominant, the distinctive mark of the inimitable technique of the Renaissance," wrote Chailley.

In defense of his thesis, Chailley cited the excellent *Lamentation de notre sainte mère l'Eglise de Constantinople*. The inspiration for this piece was the seizure of Constantinople by the infidels. The work is thought to have been performed in a luxurious production at the Fêtes du Faisan in Burgundy. It is further marked by an innovation that was to have many imitators in the years to come: With the three voices singing the French words of the lamentation, Dufay linked the liturgi-cal text of the Lamentation of Jeremiah, *Omnes amici ejus spreverunt,* sung by the tenor.

The distinctive mark of Dufay's genius lies as much in the breadth of his inspiration as in a sort of gravity and haughty dignity. These lines by Charles d'Orléans have occasionally been quoted in discussions of Dufay:

But my lips make pretense of laughter
Though many times I sense my heart weeping.

Johannes Ockeghem

Johannes Ockeghem (*ca.* 1420-1495 or 1496), like so many artistic talents of the period, came from Hainaut, and he dominated the second generation of musicians from the Belgian province.

He spent his childhood in Antwerp, where his musical education began in the cathedral choir. He became one of the twelve chaplains of the Duke of Bourbon. The appointment was short-lived, however, and from 1452 he was among the cantors of King Charles VII of France. He remained in the service of the kings of France for the rest of his life, under Louis XI and Charles VIII. Only a few journeys to Spain and Flanders interrupted his settled and well-ordered life.

His compositions quickly won him the attention

110

96

of musicians and connoisseurs. Before he reached the age of forty he was widely admired.

His death was regarded as a tragic loss by the musical aristocracy and inspired numerous poems of mourning. The most celebrated, after those of Guillaume Crétin and Erasmus, was this one, by Molinet, set to music by Josquin des Prés:

> Array yourselves in mourning robes,
> Josquin, Brumel, Pierchon*, Compère,
> Great tears let from your eyelids fall,
> Your father now is lost and gone.

Busnois composed a motet in Ockeghem's honor in his lifetime, and Johannes Tinctoris dedicated one of his treatises to him.

It may be that the universal respect of his contemporaries for Ockeghem was an extraordinary technician rather than as an inspired musician. Whatever the reason, posterity has, as a rule, confirmed the judgment of the 15th century.

Some dissent is heard, however. Ockeghem's prodigious skill as a writer has deceived some historians and has led them to characterize him as an intellectual, a simple virtuoso of counterpoint. Nothing could be further from the truth. Although

Ockeghem did leave ample and conclusive proof of his ability, his contrapuntal expertise was never an end in itself—any more than it was for Bach three centuries later.

He did, it is true, write the celebrated *Deo Gratias,* the canon for thirty-six voices that did more for his reputation than all his Masses. But according to the technicians, its construction is fundamentally simple. It is a composition for four voices, each of which supports a canon for nine voices and, Chailley says, confines itself "more or less to variation of the common chord."[33] One poet of the period compared Ockeghem to God for this particular composition.

Another of Ockeghem's masterpieces is his *Missa cujus vis toni.* Its originality lies in the absence of key, which enabled it to be sung in any of the styles then in use. It is a Mass of great musical beauty.

Ockeghem, whom one modern commentator[34] has called the Brahms of the 15th century, made use of all the forms current in his time. But it is characteristic that he should have written no more than twenty or so chansons. Although he is capable of gaiety, many of his chansons are imbued with an air of melancholy. His lament on the death of Binchois, "patron of goodness," is typical of the gravity so common in his inspiration. It is interest-

---

* Pierre de La Rue.

111

97

ing to note that in this piece Ockeghem follows the example of Dufay and combines a French text in the superius with the Latin *Miserere* in the tenor and countertenor.

The peak of Ockeghem's achievement, however, is in his religious music. He instilled in his Masses such mysticism and profound religious spirit that commentators have been led to wonder whether he was in direct contact with the Brothers of the Common Life.

In spite of the great beauty of his nine motets, his fifteen Masses are the true musical and spiritual testament of this master composer. One of the most perfect is the *Missa Mi-Mi,* or *Quarti toni,* built on a theme around a falling fifth, *mi-la* (E-A). In the Guidonian six-note scale then in use, this was *mi-mi,* hence the name.

The oldest requiem Mass still in existence was written by Ockeghem. Dufay also composed one, but no manuscripts have been preserved.

Antoine Busnois and Some Contemporaries

The names of Ockeghem and Busnois have frequently been linked, just as the names of Binchois and Dufay have been linked in the previous generation. The parallel is apt.

Antoine de Busne (?-1492), known as Busnois, was the Binchois of Charles the Bold. He accompanied the duke on some of his campaigns and was one of the creators of the court entertainments, for which he wrote more than seventy chansons.

Contemporary opinion tended to see Ockeghem and Busnois as "the two poles of musical creation, religious and secular," but to accept this is to overestimate the talents of Busnois. He is a likeable and charming composer, but superficial and, on occasion, somewhat pedantic.

The best of his work is to be found in his chansons for three voices, which have some outstanding rhythmic passages. His religious music loses true depth in an excessive pursuit of external effect. The tenor of his motet to St. Anthony, for example, consists of just one note: ray. It would appear to have been played on a bell.

Among the contemporaries of Ockeghem and Busnois, the most interesting is undoubtedly Caron, whose first name is believed to have been Philippe. His nationality, either French or Flemish, is not firmly established. We have about twenty of his chansons and a few Masses. Although the Masses fail to reveal a technique comparable to that of Ockeghem, his chansons can be counted among the most original of the age.

98

Another composer of the period was Hayne de Ghizeghem, who was in the service of the dukes of Burgundy. He, too, shone in the chanson, but only in the chanson. Others whose works have been preserved include Johannes Regis, Vincent Faugues, Jacob Barbireau and Johannes Touront. Their compositions are all religious.

Toward Humanism

The closing years of the 15th century were marked by numerous signs of an imminent, and profound, change in the conception and consideration of music. The later compositions of Josquin des Prés contain clear reflections of this mutation. To attempt to understand their meaning is to throw light at the same time on the work and personality of Josquin.

The key factor is one that, on the surface, seems uninspiring. Music, which until then had been an integral part of the *quadrivium*—that is, the mathematical disciplines—moved in the 15th century into the *trivium,* the literary disciplines.

Learning in the Middle Ages was divided between these two groups, which together comprised the "seven liberal arts." The trivium embraced grammar, rhetoric and dialectic, and from there the student went on to master arithmetic, geometry, astronomy and music, the four branches of the quadrivium.

It was a system inherited from the ancients, handed down to Christianity through the neo-Pythagorean traditions prevalent in Rome under the Empire. The Pythagoreans associated the study of music with that of arithmetic, following the lead of Pythagoras himself. Pythagoras had established the symbolism of numbers and had discovered, through his calculations, the two basic consonants of our music, the octave and the fifth.

In the sixth century the teachings of Pythagoras were adopted by Cassiodorus and by Boethius, who was considered an indisputable authority by his contemporaries. A metaphysical association was made between the doctrine of numbers and cosmic harmony that gave music a prestige it could never have achieved purely on its sonoric merits—certainly not with the theologians and the universities.

Until Josquin, then, music was essentially a mathematical art. It was based—as, indeed, it was thought the world was based—on the relationships between numbers.

Bearing this in mind, consider the work of the medieval composers. Until the end of the 15th century music makes no attempt to express individual sentiments. Its role is to reflect divine harmony.

113

Therein lies the explanation for the failure of so many music lovers to understand the pre-Renaissance masters, who, predictably, leave them unmoved. In later centuries, music was to become a confession. With Tchaikovsky it extended even into exhibitionism. But such a use of the art is quite foreign to the metaphysical nature of the Middle Ages.

Seen in this light, the vital significance of the transfer of music from the quadrivium to the trivium becomes more evident. In breaking away from numbers and their overriding symbolism to reach toward the literary disciplines, music was changing its meaning. It was moving into another world.

Henceforth music was to become the instrument of emotion and individual sentiment, a means of expression and a tool in the service of the human soul.

This process is reflected and embodied in the inspired music of Josquin des Prés, a man at the crossroads of two diametrically opposed artistic concepts.

Josquin des Prés

Little is known of the life of Josquin des Prés (*ca.* 1450-1521), who was dubbed the Prince of Musi-

cians in his own time. A native of Hainaut—again—and a choirboy at Saint-Quentin in northern France, he seems to have reached Italy at an early age. In 1474 he was in Milan, at the court of Duke Galeas Marie Sforza. Twelve years later he was in Rome, and for some eight years, at least until 1494, he was attached to the papal chapel. He was later in Florence and Ferrara and then in the chapel of Louis XII. He spent his last years at the Chapter of Condé-sur-l'Escaut in northern France, where he died.

We have, unfortunately, no knowledge of his friends and acquaintances in this age of the great masters of the Renaissance. Did he, for example, meet Leonardo da Vinci on his travels? He preceded da Vinci by only a very short time at the court of the Sforzas in Milan, and he could have met him in Rome. In Florence, did he notice a young protégé of the Medicis with the name Michelangelo? They were men of his own measure, men with an equal power of the spirit. In the one portrait we have of him, even the sad and disillusioned curl of his mouth creates a spiritual kinship with the self-portrait of the aging Leonardo or that of Michelangelo. It is a mark of the great solitary dreamers.

The work left by this man is large—some twenty Masses, a good hundred motets and nearly seventy

100

chansons. His earliest compositions are in direct line of descent from those of his predecessors from Hainaut. There are isorhythmic motets, although on analysis their character is seen to be considerably less archaic than it appears at first sight. There are Masses in which the writing and the inspiration recall the mysticism of Ockeghem.

Then, progressively, prolonged contact with Italy set Josquin free from the traditional aesthetic disciplines. He discovered among the composers south of the Alps a musical ideal distinguished from that of the north by its clarity, its symmetry, its simplicity. The quest for effect in sound was more plastic, more sensual. He saw the Italian musicians attaching a great importance to the text, using it as a model for their compositions, bending their music to its rhythm, its syntax, its accentuation. The demands of counterpoint neither dominated nor regulated the architecture of their works, and the laws of number on which the northern musicians founded their constructions—works of an unreal, diaphanous beauty as abstract as a stained glass window—had no place south of the Alps.

Josquin integrated so well with the Italian school that before long he was the master and they were the pupils. No sudden change of direction occurred in the development of his style, but it is clear that he knew where he was going.

His contemporaries certainly recognized his distinction. From the early years of the 16th century, Italian and Flemish commentators noted that Josquin was unsurpassed in his ability to project the texts of his compositions. His studies led him to create a new polyphonic style in which long notes were no more the rule in the tenor. Purely contrapuntal skills gave way to a sovereign equality and a clear transparency between the voices. Frequently they conversed with one another, two by two, freshening and underlining the words. The musical phrase abandoned ornamental arabesques and Gothic twirls for a division into periods, calm and balanced as a Renaissance façade. Chordal passages alternated with contrapuntal sequences for contrasting effect. For the first time in the history of music, a "rhetorical polyphony"[35] was created, a counterpoint regulated by the word, and no longer simply by the demands of mathematical harmony.

In general, Josquin's Masses are for four voices and reveal an exceptional variety of form and composition, each offering its own special features. Among the motets are some written for five or six voices. His chansons include compositions for from three to six voices. Some are written for voices alone, others for instruments alone, and yet others for both. And the same variety is to be found in the inspiration of his compositions.

Josquin's works form one of the purest treasures of European music. His privileged position allowed him to unite the elevated science and the profound spirituality of the Middle Ages with the first smile of the Renaissance. If the smile is tempered with a profound sadness, it is the somewhat disillusioned grandeur that is the fundamental characteristic of the work of this man, who must rank among the great masters of music.

The glow of Josquin's talent tends to throw into the shadows a number of nevertheless talented composers. Jacob Obrecht (1450-1505), in particular, is far from negligible as a musician. A Dutchman, born in Bergen-op-Zoom, he was a restless wanderer, forever changing his home and crossing back and forth over the Alps. He died of the plague in Ferrara.

His contribution to religious music was considerable. Under the influence of the Italians he wrote motets to the Virgin Mary of great sweetness. In his Masses there is a preoccupation with problems of form, which he solves, on occasion, with considerable originality. His Mass *Sub tuum praesidium,* for example, adds one voice with each new part, beginning with three and ending with seven, in a grandiose procession.

Other names worth noting are Pierre de La Rue; Antoine Brumel, who was as Italian in his work as

De La Rue was not; and Loyset Compère, a master of the chanson, a form in which he shows exuberance, humor and a gentle grace.

Germany

In view of the heights to which music was destined to climb in Germany, it is surprising to find so little eagerness among German composers to follow the lead given by France, England, Italy and Flanders. At the beginning of the century, only one name stands out—Oswald von Wolkenstein—and he, in all truth, remained very much an offshoot of the French.

The real emergence of Germany in the history of polyphony came with a blind organist from Nuremberg, Conrad Paumann (1410?-1473). Like Landino, the blind organist of Fiesole, he was expert on a number of instruments. His blindness did not prevent him from crossing the Alps several times, and in Italy he was elevated to the knighthood.

Paumann's name is inextricably linked with the beginnings of instrumental music, through a manuscript known as the *Lochamerliederbuch,* which is attributed to the circle of his pupils. It is a collection of lieder, followed by a series of transcriptions of songs and dances for keyboard instruments (the choir organ, the clavichord or the spinet), introduced by a treatise by Paumann, the *Fundamentum organisandi* (1452). It is, in fact, nothing less than a course in instrumental composition, designed to instruct the organist in the technical foundations of his craft. Yet it contains prophetic preludes, or "preambles," to an entirely new form destined for considerable growth—original composition for solo instrument.

Paumann was also the inventor of the tablature for the lute. Tablature refers to a method of notation based, not on a system of notes, but on the place of the fingers on the instrument.

The blind organist of Nuremberg trained numerous pupils, who carried his teaching abroad, and his example inspired a whole new school of organists in Germany. It was during his lifetime, in 1448, in a collection by Adam Ileborgh, that the use of the pedal was indicated for the first time.

At the end of the 15th century, all the forms that the succeeding centuries were to develop were already present, and in strength. The instrumental dances, the transcriptions of dancing songs and the first compositions for solo instrument were to give birth to the suite, and then the sonata and the symphony. And the entremets so beloved of the courts offered the first glimpse of the opera and ballet to come.

*101 Group of angels,
including musicians playing
the harp and the flute.
Detail from the "Coronation
of the Virgin" by an
unidentified painter of the
Cologne school referred to
as the Master of the
Life of Mary (ca. 1463-1480)*

Notes

1-3   In particular, the very well documented work by Walter Salmen, The Traveling Musician in Middle Ages Europe, Kassel, 1960.

4-5   Gallimard Encyclopedia.

6   Walter Salmen, op. cit.

7   Muset, 13th-century French poet, specialized in courtly songs. Quoted in Life in the Time of St. Louis, Edmond Faral, Hachette, 1938.

8   Walter Salmen, op. cit.

9-12 Edmond Faral, op. cit.

13   Walter Salmen.

14   Karl Nef, History of Music, Payot.

15   Figures quoted by Walter Salmen.

16   Hans Engel, Music and Society, Berlin, 1960.

17   Quoted by Jacques Chailley, Musical History of the Middle Ages.

18-19 Gustave Cohen, The Great Clarity of the Middle Ages, EMF, 1943.

20   For more information on technical details, see Musical Notation by Armand Machabey, PUF.

21   Jacques Chailley makes a detailed analysis of them.

22   Gustave Cohen, op. cit.

23   O. Cartellieri, The Court of the Dukes of Burgundy, Payot, 1946.

24   According to O. Cartellieri.

25   Hans Engel, op. cit.

26-29 O. Cartellieri, op. cit.

30   G. Thibault, Gallimard Encyclopedia.

31   J. Karl Huysmans.

32   Nanie Bridgman, Gallimard Encyclopedia.

33   Jacques Chailley, op. cit.

34   Charles Van den Borren, Belgian music and art critic.

35   H. Osthoff in New Musical Journal, 1962.

Suggested List of Records

Abbreviations:
AM: Amadeo
A.P.: Archiv-Produktion
CAM: Camerata
CHR: Christophorus
E: Erato
H.M.: Harmonia Mundi
L: Lumen
TEL: Telefunken
VAL: Valois

13th century. Music of the Middle Ages and the beginning of the Renaissance, 13th and 14th centuries

Mass for three voices
(known as the Tournai Mass),
13th and 14th centuries,
dir. Marc Honegger. ☐ L.

Carmina Burana: from the original manuscript (**ca.** 1300), Münchener Marienknaben, dir. K. Rith. ☐ TEL.

13th, 15th and 17th centuries,
Mariengesänge: Ave Virgo Virginum,
by the Capella Antiqua of Munich. ☐ CHR.

Chansons and motets of the 13th century,
by Pro Musica Antiqua,
dir. Safford Cape. ☐ A.P.

17 dances of the 13th and 14th centuries,
by Pro Musica Antiqua,
dir. S. Cape. ☐ A.P.

8 madrigals and caccia taken from Antonio Squarcialupi's Codex,
by Pro Musica Antiqua,
dir. S. Cape. ☐ A.P.

Adam de La Halle:
Le Jeu de Robin et Marion (13 rondeaus),
by Pro Musica Antiqua,
dir. S. Cape. ☐ A.P.

Musica Navalis Pragensis in Honorem
Sancti Joannis Nepomuceni,
Ensemble Pro Arte Antiqua, Prague. ☐ H.M.

14th century

Guillaume de Machaut:
Messe Notre-Dame ("for the Coronation
of Charles V"). ☐ H.M.

Messe Notre-Dame,
by Pro Musica Antiqua, dir. S. Cape. ☐ A.P.

Messe Notre-Dame,
the Paris vocal and instrumental ensemble,
dir. R. Blanchard. ☐ TEL.

10 secular works,
dir. R. Blanchard. ☐ A.P.

Francesco Landino: 4 madrigals,
by Pro Musica Antiqua,
dir. S. Cape. ☐ A.P.

Oswald von Wolkenstein: 11 lieder,
by the Jugendmusikschule of Hanover,
dir. W. Träder. ☐ A.P.

Ludus Paschalis (Liturgical setting of
the Passion,
14th century, restored by Ch. Ravier),
by the Paris Ensemble Polyphonique,
dir. Ch. Ravier. ☐ VAL.

15th century

Carols, Old English Processional Hymns:
  Synge we to thir mery cumpane.
  Go day, my Lord.
  Eya martir Stephen.
  Deo gracies Anglia.
by Pro Musica Sacra and the
Ensemble of Mediaeval Instruments,
dir. Bruno Turner. ☐ A.P.

Josquin des Prés:
Messe Pange Lingua,
by the Ensemble Caillard. ☐ E.

Josquin des Prés:
Missa Hercules Dux Ferrariae—Motette
Misericordias Domini, by the St. Eustache
singers and instrumental ensemble, dir.
R. P. Emile Martin. Coll. Musica
Sacra. ☐ AM.

Josquin des Prés:
Grande Virgo, mater Christi
(Palestrina-Kreis),
dir. Franz Clausing. ☐ CHR.

Josquin des Prés:
8 secular compositions,
by Pro Musica Antiqua,
dir. S. Cape. ☐ A.P.

Josquin des Prés:
Geistliche Werke,
by Capella Antiqua of Munich. ☐ TEL.

Josquin des Prés:
Christmas motets,
by the Ensemble Hilversum,
dir. M. Voorberg. ☐ CAM.

John Dunstable:
6 motets,
by Pro Musica Antiqua,
dir. S. Cape. ☐ A.P.

John Dunstable:
Quam pulcra es,
by the Capella Antiqua of Munich. ☐ TEL.

Music at the court of Burgundy:
(Ockeghem, Dufay, De Lantins, Obrecht,
Morton, Binchois) by Pro Musica Antiqua,
Brussels, dir. S. Cape. ☐ AM.

Guillaume Dufay:
5 religious songs, 3 religious songs,
by Pro Musica Antiqua, dir. S. Cape. ☐ A.P.

Guillaume Dufay:
"Ad coenam agni," Capella Antiqua
of Munich;
Homme Armé Mass,
by the Paris vocal and instrumental
ensemble,
dir. R. Blanchard. ☐ TEL.

Guillaume Dufay:
Masses (extracts)—Motets and Hymns,
by the Capella Antiqua of Munich. ☐ TEL.

Johannes Ockeghem:
5 chansons,
by Pro Musica Antiqua,
dir. S. Cape. ☐ A.P.

Johannes Ockeghem:
Agnus Dei I, II, III extracts
from the Missa Mi-Mi,
Capella Antiqua of Munich. ☐ TEL.

Jacob Obrecht:
Parce, Domini, for three voices
Parce, Domini, for four voices;
by Capella Antiqua of Munich. TEL.

Jacob Obrecht:
12 chansons of the Renaissance,
by the Ensemble Ph. Caillard. ☐ E.

102 *Ass playing the organ.*
(Choirstall in the Marienkirche
at Lübeck—second half of
the 14th century)

We wish to thank all those people and institutions that have made this work possible, in particular Suzanne Patrick; Renate Wulff; Roger Ségalat; Wolf Strobel; Hans Ulrich Kerth; the National Library, Paris; the Library and Museum of Decorative Arts, Paris; the Bavarian State Library, Munich; and the German National Museum, Nuremberg.

The illustrations and documents, represented by figure numbers, come from the following public and private collections:

Library of the Arsenal, Paris: 20, 21, 53.

National Library, Paris: 27, 31, 33, 34, 36-38, 46-48, 58, 64, 66-70, 72-74, 77, 78, 96, 99, 100.

Library and Museum of Decorative Arts, Paris: 1-3, 19, 24, 26, 40, 49 and the unnumbered illustrations in the Suggested List of Records.

National Conservatory of Music, Paris: 97, 98.

Condé Museum, Chantilly: 50-52, 55.

The Louvre, Paris: 84-86.

Versailles Museum: 71.

Royal Library, Brussels: 14, 15.

British Museum, London: 29, 79-81.

O. Reinhart collection, Winterthur: 94.

Art and History Archives, Berlin: 61.

Collection of Copper Plate Engravings, Berlin: 25.

Bavarian National Museum, Munich: 9, 10.

Bavarian State Library, Munich: 41, 42, 45.

German Museum, Munich: 56.

State Picture Collection, Munich: 83, 101.

German National Museum, Nuremberg: 11, 26, 44.

Bärenreiter Picture Archives, Kassel: 12, 22, 23, 53, 54.

Picture Archives, Marbourg: 4, 6-8, 13, 39, 62, 63, 65, 76, 82, 88, 94, 103.

Castelli, Lübeck: 75, 102.

Kerth, Munich: 9-11, 14-18, 26, 30, 43, 44, 57, 59, 93, 95.

Schroll Press, Vienna-Munich: 87.

Bulloz, Paris: 20, 21.

Giraudon, Paris: 50-52, 55, 71, 84-86, 89-92.

Viollet, Paris: 5.

Acknowledgments

103 *Idiot wearing a bell cap.*
(Choirstall in the church of
St. Peter in Louvain, Belgium)

103